# TRIUMPH OVER FEAR

# TRIUMPH OVER FEAR

by

## D. M. WILSON

LONDON
VICTOR GOLLANCZ LTD
1966

*Printed in Great Britain by*
*The Camelot Press Ltd., London and Southampton*

TO ALL
WHO ARE BATTLING
AGAINST FEAR

# CONTENTS

# ACKNOWLEDGMENTS

The author gratefully acknowledges permission to quote, as follows:

Lady Dunsany (*The Donnellan Lectures*); Mlle Oriel Malet (*Marraine*); Faber & Faber, Ltd and "Nicodemus" (*Renascence*); Chatto and Windus, Ltd and Mr. James Strachey (*Eminent Victorians*); Chatto and Windus and the Executors of Aldous Huxley (*The Song of God*); John Murray, Ltd and Mr. Patrick Leigh Fermor (*A Time to Keep Silence*); Basil Blackwell & Mott, Ltd and Mr. F. T. H. Fletcher (*Pascal and the Mystical Tradition*); Constable & Co., Ltd and Dr. Helen Waddell (*The Wandering Scholars*); The Society for Promoting Christian Knowledge and His Grace the Archbishop of Canterbury (*Image Old and New*); Peter Davies, Ltd and the Executors of the Rev. Brian Hession (*Determined to Live*); Methuen & Co., Ltd and the Executors of Oscar Wilde (*De Profundis*); Methuen & Co., Ltd and the Executors of Rufus Jones (*The Faith and Practice of Quakers*); Burns & Oates, Ltd and Mr. Algar Thorold (translator) (*Self-Abandonment to Divine Providence*—de Caussade); Oxford University Press and Dr. F. A. Iremonger (*Biography of William Temple*); George Allen & Unwin, Ltd and (*a*) Dr. Radhakrishnan (*Recovery of Faith* and *Eastern Religion and Western Thought*), (*b*) Executors of President Masaryk (*President Masaryk tells his Story*), (*c*) Dr. A. Guirdham (*A Theory of Disease*); Hogarth Press, Ltd and the Executors of Rainer Maria Rilke and the Executors of J. B. Leishman (translator) (*Requiem*); Hodder and Stoughton, Ltd and Dr. Leslie D. Weatherhead (*Psychology, Religion and Healing*); *Science of Thought Review* and the Executors of H. T. Hamblin and Miss Clare Cameron (*My Search for Truth* and *Science of Thought Review*, respectively); Longmans, Green & Co., Ltd and the Executors of Dean Inge (*Personal Religion and the Life of Devotion*); Collins, Publishers and (*a*) Sir Arthur Bryant (*The Age of Chivalry*), (*b*) Executors of Gerald Vann (*The Son's Course*), (*c*) Executors of Pierre Teilhard de Chardin and Sir Julian Huxley (*The Phenomenon of Man*), Executors of Pierre Teilhard de Chardin (*Le Milieu Divin*), (*d*) Executors of C. G. Jung (*Dreams, Memories, Reflections*); Routledge and Kegan Paul, Ltd and (*a*) Executors of C. G. Jung (*Modern Man in Search of a Soul*), (*b*) Victor White (*God and the Unconscious*); S.C.M. Press, Ltd and Dr. Alan Richardson (*Christian Apologetics*); Macmillan & Co. Ltd and Mrs. William Temple (*Readings in St. John's Gospel*); Penguin Books, Ltd and (*a*) Clifton Wolters (translator) (*The Cloud of Unknowing*), (*b*) Executors of Beatrice Webb (*My Apprenticeship*), (*c*) Leo Shirley-Price (translator) (*The Imitation of Christ*), (*d*) J. M. Cohen (translator) (*Life of St. Teresa of Avila*); Sheed & Ward, Ltd, and (*a*) Executors of Dom John Chapman (*Spiritual Letters*), (*b*) F. J. Sheed (*Man, the Forgotten*); Hamish Hamilton, Ltd and (*a*) Miss Monica Baldwin (*I leap over the wall*), (*b*) Miss Helen Hayes (*What I believe*); Geoffrey Bles, Ltd and (*a*) Executors of N. Berdyaev (*Freedom and the Spirit*), (*b*) Rev. J. B. Phillips (*Letters to Young Churches*), (*c*) Executors of C. S. Lewis (*George Macdonald, an Anthology*); The Christian Frontier Council and (*a*) Erland Sundstrom (*Dag Hammarskjold*), (*b*) R. A. Lambourne (*What is healing?*); The *Observer* and Sir Julian Huxley (*Religion without God*); Harper & Row, Ltd and Mr. Walter T. Stace (*The Teachings of the Mystics*); *The Burrswood Herald* and the Bishop of Birmingham (*Suffering*); Jonathan Cape, Ltd, and (*a*) the Executors of the J. W. M. Sullivan Estate (*Beethoven*), (*b*) Mr. Kenneth Walker (*Meaning and Purpose*).

# I

## CATASTROPHE

Catastrophe is a movement down upon or away from the normal course of mortal life. The oldest associations of the terms "strophe," "antistrophe" and "catastrophe" are musical. "Strophe" and "antistrophe" are the stroke and the counter-stroke, the refrain and the antiphony, the utterance and the echo of our human chorus; "catastrophe" is that which strikes down upon and athwart that mortal with an immortal music, creating to ears unattuned to it, cacophony and discord.—In its root significance catastrophe thus implies transcendent power, the rhythm of some reality remote from our mundane and diurnal reality, intervening suddenly and unpredictably into the rhythm of our history, shattering the previous pattern of our lives and days.

"NICODEMUS"

WHEN THE CATASTROPHE enveloped us, Dorfs was a normally healthy woman of sixty, full of life and laughter, nearly as supple as an adolescent, her body disciplined by years of classical dancing. She had had nearly forty years of married happiness, busy years, with her full share of struggle and problems, and she was facing exciting new horizons—my gradual retirement emerging as the prelude to more leisure, new interests and the changed tempo of living which retirement makes practicable.

After a few months of aches and pains she was examined by a specialist, taken to hospital for anxious weeks of tests. Two years later she died.

This is an account, not of illness, nor of recovery, but of response to a challenge and of its consequences. The consequences include much re-thinking, on many subjects. Some of it emerged as the day-to-day world receded more and more, and our participation in it became not only less, but less desired. A great deal of it was the outcome of intuitive processes, our sharing being unquestioned, mutually recognized for its sureness. Later, in the misty period when I was alone, shaping a new life, the totally different pattern, partly woven during the long ordeal, resulted in new valuations and re-thinking as some sort of personal philosophy for living.

The heroic episode of a sufferer's triumph may have significance for other sufferers and for the tortured minds of many who spend their days caring for them. The re-thinking is recorded as a direct result of partial withdrawal, forced solitude and looking at the human procession from the sidelines.

"Interpreters," a friend was saying, "interpreters, we need them so badly, to supplement the books which seldom deal factually, personally, with the strange experiences such as you have had." He went on to stress the need to interpret for the ordinary reader, for the non-scientific, non-technical mind, for whom there are not a sufficient number of first-hand accounts of challenge accepted positively and of the re-valuations when the ordeal left a partner—not stranded, but on firm ground, free from the ravages of emotional turmoil.

Forced withdrawal over a long period provides not only mental space but spaciousness. "It is unavoidable," wrote Lord Dunsany, "that the things at our doors, the things that are daily about us, should attract our attention more urgently than the force of eternal laws or the calm of the stars; and I have even noticed that in a tent in a desert a contemplation of the way we are going, and perhaps some estimate of it, is easier than when one is walking among the dust of that way. And I think that as many philosophies which man has made for his guidance have come out of deserts as from the cities in which he mostly dwells; and when you come to religions, the desert claims nearly all of them. It would almost seem that the seeds of immortality need not the plough and the fertile acres for their sowing, or showers of rain to moisten them, but the dry and sandy desert and the calm of remote stars."[1]

We came to know "the calm of remote stars" or at any rate, the calm induced by much gazing, and "desert" in the sense of isolation was an atmosphere which more and more we found nourishing. The busy streets, the clamour and the lights of the city, and all its gaiety, gently, very gradually receded. Nature can be very gentle in transferring us from one world to another. Of that we were to learn a great deal.

But first we were to learn that man has no rights in his imagined security. In how few moments can its bulwarks be undermined! It seemed as if a tottering spire came crashing through our shuddering roof, walls meeting as they collapsed into the wreckage; everything smudged, smeared, senseless, silly. Chaos. "I have to tell you," the specialist said, to me alone, when the diagnosis was clear, "that we have had no cures." He knew we wanted the whole truth.

Looking back, that seems like the first milestone along a road which ended in serenity and in triumph. Viewed that morning, it seemed to plunge into fog and unquiet loneliness. How vividly, in seconds, the frightened mind can compass a long journey —the groping, the near-exhaustion, nerves twisted, emotion squeezed, the human spirit continuing to exist only because it is forbidden to die. Nothing to fight against, no direction, nothing but—nothing.

I left the hospital, dazed.

"First," I said to myself, "walk; find your feet. Don't try to think. Wrestling with problems at this moment won't get you anywhere. Somehow you have to be calm. This afternoon you have to tell Dorfs. In the split second between pushing her door open and greeting her she will have searched your face, gimlet eyes will penetrate deep into your very being. Tranquillity. That is imperative. Steer clear of self-pity. What are you going to say? Not yet. That will come. Don't press it. How much will she know already? What has her real assessment added up to? And that intuitive sense, in her so devastatingly accurate—and what about her subconscious,"—so I argued with myself. I was submerged.

With no plan, knowing lunch to be out of the question, I wandered on and found I had arrived at a Roman Catholic Church. We are Protestants. I went inside. Perhaps if I could kneel, in stillness, I might find my way. I suppose that as long as I live I shall now and then hear "Rock of Ages" sung to a tune I had not heard since boyhood. Apparently a closing hymn. I remained kneeling when the little congregation filed out. Altar candles were snuffed, everyone gone, deep quiet.

Sometimes the impossible task in sick visiting turns out to be completely free from problems. Is it guidance? Acceptance? Or the realization of such utter helplessness that an instinctive kind of trust brings one, in inscrutable ways, to the right words, the unfaltering voice, the mental poise?

I began to feel that all would work out in some way which would not overwhelm us. Prolonged tests had indicated that the outcome might be serious. That we knew. An observation period gives some slight degree of protection from shock. As I began to walk back I had a strange feeling, nothing short of conviction, that Dorfs would triumph over fear. Of her courage I had no doubt. In crises and in illnesses she had always been magnificent. I realized that what had terrified me most was the fear of my own clumsiness; I prayed that my courage and calm might be patterned on hers.

When I opened her door all doubt was dissipated by the reassurance in her eyes and the understanding in her smile. Very simply, I told her. She caught the significant phrase out of the detailed description of the complaint, just as I knew she would. We were stunned and mystified and we recognized that the mystery was shattering, involving a life commitment and a life sentence. But Dorfs' response to the challenge was instantaneous, positive, uncompromising. "This," she said, oh, so calmly, so humbly, "this is where we begin."

Accepting what she would never resign herself to, she set our pattern. She would fight the insidious disease, sure of her doctor, her specialist, her family. It was a baffling assignment; if it were humanly possible, by striving and in faith and in humility, she would win. There must be research going on and medical research has virtually eliminated one disease after another. One day, one patient was cured; the story of the conquest of any disease is in two parts, before and after the first successful treatments have been found. No reason why, equipped as she was and above all, undeterred, positive, unresenting, fighting backed by faith, she would not co-operate with medical science, give research the fullest opportunities and be cured.

Muscular complaints are so diverse as to be beyond classification by the layman. Thousands of sufferers, physically limited by muscular disability, live happily for many years, cheerfully making terms with a life restricted in movement and achieving marvels which are humbling to people of normal muscular capacity. The diagnosis showed Dorfs to be suffering from progressive muscular atrophy, a relatively rare form of muscular trouble and hitherto unknown to us; we had heard of muscular dystrophy, a totally different form of muscular disease which has records of many years of astonishing achievements by sufferers. It attacks a much larger number of people than atrophy; rightly, research in that field has priority. So we were compelled to realize that research focussed specifically on the particular form of disease with which we were concerned was non-existent.

Facing an ordeal of this kind, aware not only that there had been no cures but that there was no specific research, is stern indeed. Through resentment and rebellion or alternatively, through acceptance and co-operation, you must in any event be changed. Your world becomes a different world; nothing can be the same again. It is a gradual process; Nature abhors haste. But the completeness of the change is inevitable. Dorfs' experience proved all over again that if you can accept this change and co-operate, fear can be transmuted into a strange light which radiates beyond suffering, maybe even beyond time.

# II

# FEAR

There is no room for fear in love; perfect love banishes fear.

1 JOHN 4: 18 (NEW ENGLISH BIBLE)

FEAR, IN THIS book, means the ghoulish thing that can disintegrate your very being. Hovering like an evil spirit, crashing like a crag hurtling down a ravine, terror is too mild a name for it. You are petrified, submerged, and most poignant of all, you feel utterly alone, abandoned, with demons screeching, your own sanity questioned, head and heart bursting, relentlessly tearing you to pieces, nerve gone. Stunned and reeling, you are sick at heart, humiliated, prostrated, despair confronting you. The bottom has dropped out of your world.

Other kinds of fear are totally different. Fear that is awe. "The fear of the Lord is the beginning of wisdom." The discipline of fear that can save us from many a blunder, just as pain, one of Nature's signals, can, by warning us, protect our health.

But as used here, fear is evil. Fear that has its roots in self-depreciation, that arch-enemy of humility; fear that is a focus on failure; fear that is obsessional remorse; fear that is a blind conviction of hopelessness, ultimately even wallowing in it; fear that is the bedfellow of endless brooding; the fear of the drug addict, the sex addict, the alcoholic; fear of facing one's self, and still worse, fear of facing reality.

For so often, facing reality dispels fear and sets us on the road to ultimate triumph. This, Dorfs showed us. Her first step was to face reality. What it cost her, no one can know; we know that it cost nothing compared with the incalculable cost of refusing to face reality. Instead of bitterness or resentment, there came the serenity born of positive acceptance; what must otherwise have ended in humiliating defeat became a triumph. Instead of vacillation, the dynamic sweep of decision flung wide the gates; instead of dallying or bargaining with God, there was surrender into the immensity of that invincible power which no one understands. We who witnessed it all needed no definition. For fear, this evil thing, can bring us to heightened reverence. Beyond reverence there is a way opening. Strangely, it is a way to freedom, however hopeless the tragedy may seem.

Fear of fear is its own magnetizing, just as brooding on vice gives it fangs and fire. Fear challenged, is, by the alchemy of the challenge, fused into part of our perfecting; due to the challenge we can be changed. Through something beyond our fashioning we can surrender into kinship with the divine.

In grave illness, fear can begin as a haunting, ravaging, senseless thing, a diabolical and devouring evil, yet there is no more human example of evil that can be used for good—changed into good; as we were to discover, what can happen is not only that fear can eventually be succeeded by good, but far more significantly, fear can in some mysterious way become a factor in building what ultimately emerges as nothing less than triumph. So fear can be an ordeal which, like a crucible, is for refining, proving gold to be gold. The shattering thing which could undermine the whole edifice of your living and destroy whatever you have garnered as philosophy, this can, even by its own defeat, subsequently help to strengthen your faith and to re-build it if you have lost it. And if you have to operate from a narrowed base, this can be essential for the broadening of your activities. In this sense, the corroding aspect of fear can be transmuted into radiance. Radiance so infectious as to imply new dimensions of living.

Triumph over fear is accomplished by the invasion of love, fear's mortal foe. Love and fear will battle for the domination of your life, and so long as love is hesitant, reserved or uncertain, fear can overwhelm you. It will in any event win some battles. War consists of battles won and lost, both winning and losing being inevitable in human affairs. But if you are so invaded by love that it possesses you, it becomes dynamic, and through arduous enduring, much suffering and many trials, in which it becomes battle-scarred, love triumphs over fear. Nothing else can. Nothing short of this invading, dynamic love can survive the sinister, insidious attacks of fear, which delude us into self-pity, dinning into half-reluctant ears that we haven't deserved the calamity and the tragedy, bidding us rebel, landing us, save for the dynamic of love, in bitter resentment. And resentment is a road to defeat.

Without humility, none of this is possible, the real humility which is selflessness. Selfless, we are somehow freed from dread, yet this is part of the daily encounter. Like liberty, like faith, humility has to be won every day. Triumph over fear is a daily triumph. Fear cannot be banished permanently, and the humble, claiming no triumph, know only too intimately, how true this is. "There is no day," wrote Dorfs to a friend, "when there is no battle." Desolation threatening, human frailty all too pervading —triumph is the only word to describe what is so much more than survival, or even winning; a complete reversal, the enemy not only overcome, but routed.

Real humility admits the analogy of the block of marble and the sculptor; we are the marble, no longer either claiming to be the sculptor or guessing the ultimate design.

Real humility knows no resentment; rights forgotten, life becomes a succession of privileges, vibrant, magnanimous, freed from all that is carping, negative, devitalising.

Real humility is the triumph over the ego, man's Enemy Number Two, fear being Number One.

# III

## NON-MEDICAL HEALING

In the First World War a young doctor, working in the desert amongst troops stationed north of Baghdad, talked about his dreams to two young chaplains far into the night. I was one of the chaplains.

That doctor was a remarkable man. He practised psychological treatment of an impressive kind when what was then called "The New Psychology" was very new indeed. He practised hypnotism, both as a means of investigating the deep mind of the patient and also of giving him suggestions of courage, confidence and recovery. Further, he had as great a spiritual faith and power as I have ever seen. He would go out into the desert, and for hours he would concentrate his mind on one patient with a kind of spiritual intention. On returning he would sometimes find remarkable results. The patient, previously sleepless, would be asleep; or, discontented, would have found peace of mind; or, in despair, had begun to believe in his own recovery. In one case, a man apparently unable to walk was walking about the ward. The doctor claimed that when he had done all he could for a patient by all the arts of medicine, the turning point in the illness was sometimes determined by adding this form of prayerful concentration. . . . When this doctor turned to us two chaplains and said, "You padres ought to be doing most of this," I felt he was right. . . . I therefore determined to learn all I could about non-physical ways of healing.

DR. LESLIE D. WEATHERHEAD

WHEN MEDICAL SCIENCE says "we have had no cures," non-medical healing takes first priority in one's thinking. In common with thousands of people, we had had for many years a rather vague, general interest in the subject. Between the two world wars personal friends had investigated, in great detail over a prolonged period, numerous healings relating to an amazing diversity of complaints, resulting from the "odic gift," as it is called, of a man not in any way associated with religion or spiritual influence. During those middle years, too, we had a friend who, to use his own words, had been up and down Harley Street for years. Then he became a Christian Scientist; we were in a position to vouch for the fact that for the next twenty years he saw no doctor, took no medicine, and enjoyed good health. We then lost touch with the family; but he lived to over eighty years of age. A friend knocked about in the First World War had in the succeeding years continuing ill-health so serious that it seemed likely he would not be able to work at all. Doctors seemed unable to help. After a number of treatments by a spiritualist he regained sound health, worked and lived normally into old age. We had a friend who was regarded in his middle years as a miracle, surviving an illness which is regarded as a killer. In his old age, he told us that he would not hesitate to see a doctor if he felt the need of medical attention; his belief in medical science was profound. He was a dedicated man. Living a selfless life, he derived daily sustenance through prayer and devotion to his God. We readily accepted his word that for more than a dozen years he saw no doctor, took no medicine.

Shortly after we received the real diagnosis of Dorfs' complaint, we discovered that a man, who, to our knowledge, had been under medical treatment for ulcers for nearly a year, had visited a faith-healer and apparently been cured; five years later, there has been no recurrence of the trouble.

None of these instances is remarkable; there are thousands like them. They are quoted only because we knew the patients and the circumstances personally. Remembering them as we faced our problem, we began to think, to read, to investigate, to listen, to try to find out what the wise thing could be *for us* to do. For at the outset we both realized the significance of the personal factor. If everyone could be cured by becoming Christian Scientists or Spiritualists, by going to Lourdes, or to faith-healers—that is too elementary to need an answer. It doesn't work like that.

Yet miracles can happen. Mystery is mystery, nor without mystery could there be miracles, essentially and by their very nature outside the power of the human intelligence to comprehend. No section of the community has in recent years shown itself more ready to acknowledge the limitations of brain and of science than our medical men; privileged, as few are, to witness the activities of the human spirit long after intelligence has been ready to acknowledge defeat, they have now and then discovered, to their amazement, a turn which has become a healing, unaccountable and subsequently proved not to be a short-term rallying. In humility, wise doctors tell us that some things are beyond normal experience. This perpetual encouragement for every sufferer is armour against invading despair. The powers of science are finite; divine power is illimitable.

So we resolved not to panic. We would try to use our intelligence. Tact was needed in framing non-committal but genuinely grateful letters to anxious friends, so very willing to help, in so many different ways.

One of the heartening discoveries to the lay student is that medical science appears to be so much more open-minded than it was in the early years of this century, particularly in its relationships with religion, which means mainly, but not exclusively, with the churches.

"In a sense, all healing may be considered to be divine. Many aspects of healing are still outside our present knowledge and this we should humbly admit."

"The spiritual healer may succeed where the physician, particularly if untrained in the recognition and treatment of psychological illness, may fail."

"Health may be described as a condition of satisfactory functioning of the whole organism. The words *health, wholeness* and *holiness* are closely linked in origin."

"Recent progress in medicine has shown that physical health depends on more than physical agents."

"Health is more than a physical problem and the patient's attitude, both to illness and to other problems, is an important factor in his recovery and adjustment to life."

"It would seem that the whole field of medical practice in relation to the work of the church should be explored."

"The more nearly the whole man is or can be treated, the more complete will be the healing."

These extracts[1] from a report issued by the British Medical Association in 1956 indicate realistic groping towards co-operation; several years after the report was issued, "groping" is still not an unsuitable word to describe the situation, but "realistic" is equally appropriate. We were specifically encouraged when we read in this report that "the more nearly the whole man is or can be treated the more complete will be the healing." But to anyone confronted with catastrophe, as we were, the most significant passage was this:

"Medical men not infrequently meet with illness which, as far as previous experience goes, should prove fatal, but which appears to resolve unexpectedly. There are reports of cancers behaving in this way. These cures take place apart from medical or surgical treatment and without special ministrations of other kinds such as "spiritual healing." These cures are at the present

time inexplicable and not enough is known about the processes to enable anyone to say exactly what has happened."

If that paragraph means anything, it means that a patient is
never justified in giving up hope. Later, the same report says:
". . . several doctors stated that spontaneous cures had occurred
in malignant disease."

Towards the end of the report the relationship of medicine and
the church was defined unambiguously:

> "As man is body, mind and spirit, and health depends upon
> the harmonious functioning of the whole man, the tasks of
> medicine and the church are inseparable."

In 1953 there had been set up by the Archbishops of Canterbury
and York a Commission charged with the investigation of this
all-important subject of co-operation between physician and
priest. Its terms of reference were wide, maybe too wide; its
report, not issued until 1958, was lengthy, touching on debatable
aspects of complex problems. Comments on the work of the
Commission, as reported in the press, included the following:

> "The Bishop of Coventry said healing did not always follow
> faith, as was so frequently thought, nor was suffering always
> contrary to God's will."

> "The Bishop of Rochester said he was assured by 'those who
> know' that at least one-third of the patients occupying beds in
> hospitals were really sufferers who needed the ministry of an
> expert priest and not the services of a doctor."

Which brought to mind Jung's oft-quoted statement, "Among all
my patients in the second half of life—that is to say, over thirty-
five—there has not been one whose problem in the last resort was
not that of finding a religious outlook on life."

A much less-known quotation from Jung, relevant here, is:

"Christ is in us and we are in him! Why should the activity of God and the presence of the Son of Man within us not be real and observable? Every day I am thankful to God that I have been allowed to experience the reality of the Divine Image within me . . . thanks to this act of grace, my life has meaning. . . ."[2]

In a booklet entitled *The Place of Healing in the Ministry of the Church*, the Rev. George Macleod, Leader of the Iona Community, reports a doctor's statement to him—"Sixty per cent of my patients are really looking for the confessional," and in the same booklet he quotes the opinion of the Superintendent of one of our largest asylums that "well over fifty per cent could leave tomorrow if we could convince them of their forgiveness." Dr. Arthur Guirdham, writing as a psychiatrist, emphasizes that whilst "health is a by-product of religious experience . . . the sick cannot successfully embrace religion with the aim of gaining health in the process." We recognized that to be confirmation of what we both believed. Dr. Guirdham continues—"The individual who takes himself to religion to obtain relief from his psychosomatic illness will almost invariably be doomed to disappointment. In seeking positively his own health he is encumbered by an awareness of self which is liable to act as a guarantee of the continuance of his malady. Health is the incidental product arising from the process of self-annihilation. In this, as in other spheres, he who loses his life will save it and who saves his life will lose it."[3] Later in the same book he says:

"Only a small minority of mankind can be said to achieve continuing happiness. For the majority, happiness is incidental. —It involves not self-awareness, but being lost.—The active phase of being lost occurs whenever man is truly and without reservations absorbed in what he is doing for the sake of what Kipling called the Thing, and without consideration of any profit, material, social, mental, or even spiritual, for himself."

"The vital undercurrent of our being is dedicated to the annihilation of ourselves as personalities, in the thrustful, driving, obsessional sense of the term."

". . . many people so dedicated are busy about their daily affairs and leading what appears to be an ordinary social existence, but with this difference, that, whereas before, they confronted their daily tasks as a challenge to their personalities, they now offer themselves to the same occupations as instruments of the Infinite."

In a series of articles devoted to the spiritual aspects of healing, which appeared in the *Nursing Times* in 1959, one concise statement calls for quotation here.[4]

"Today it is realized that medical treatment alone is inadequate to cure sickness of which the cause may well be found in the soul rather than in the body."

This recognition of inadequacy is stated in a different and very concise way in a pamphlet published by the Christian Medical Fellowship and edited by two medical men, Dr. Vincent Edmunds and Dr. C. Gordon Scorer, which opens as follows:[5]

"Both the process of recovering from an illness and the healing of wounded or diseased tissues alike remain a mystery."

One is reminded of what was said about Florence Nightingale at a time—in the Crimean War—when medical services on a foreign battlefield were primitive as well as inadequate. "Over and over again," wrote Lytton Strachey, "her untiring efforts rescued those whom the surgeons had abandoned as beyond the possibility of cure." No wonder he could add that "a passionate idolatry spread among the men; they kissed her shadow as she passed."[6] Faith-healing in splendid interpretation, surely.

Separated from, yet surely a part of non-medical healing, are what may be called "channels of help." Help which can be quite invaluable but which makes no claim to cure; help, therefore, received and welcomed for what it is. Some instances which we found helpful should be mentioned here—partly in recognition and gratitude, partly because others may be helped.

Two people unknown to each other wrote to say that they would particularly like to think of Dorfs at a specific time each day, not asking for anything to be done at our end; since we believed that a receptive mind could (in ways unknown to us) heighten the intensity of anything which might accrue, we co-operated fully. We were careful not to think in terms of results or improvements or anything beyond an acceptance of the idea that thought can affect other people.

We had no personal experience of prayer groups. A friend brought us the experience without our joining any group, but we co-operated gratefully, always avoiding thinking in terms of results. We were advised of the date and time of a monthly service of prayer at which Dorfs would be specifically remembered, "It is most helpful," Dorfs wrote to this friend, "to have the time of your service and a very necessary humbling experience to realize its full implications. So much beauty is being revealed that I count myself thrice blessed and on the grey days find that strength comes through, and upholding in the thoughts of friends. . . . Though the physical condition is worsening, I am very conscious of all the help which is coming from many sources, some unknown, realizing that I am but a vehicle and must accept (without being resigned) what may not be understood. . . . Be sure that we believe all works towards good."

It is a privilege to record, in deep gratitude, the help of friends who assured us at various times that we were in their thoughts and in their prayers. Prayer cannot be adequately investigated by the orthodox methods of science. Nor can thought; but research compels us to recognize (a) the transference of thought, and (b) the potency of focussed thought, as no longer in question.

In the early months following the diagnosis we talked many

B

times about these various aspects of non-medical healing. Non-medical healing Dorfs never challenged, nor did I; the factual evidence is too overwhelming for challenge to be intelligent. We realized, too, from our enquiries and our reading that non-medical healing cannot be explained by any scientific formula. In the physical sense, some are healed, some are not. We considered the possible drift into despair of those who might resort to non-medical healers as a last hope, believing that they might believe. The effectiveness of any form of non-medical healing— and indeed, medical healing in many cases—is partly, and sometimes largely dependent on our own believing; the soundness of this becomes more apparent if we reverse the idea—go to non-medical healers disbelieving, and it seems doubtful, judging by records, if benefits would accrue.

Faith is a variable element, not only in degree but in type; the published accounts of non-medical healing encourage the theory that patients whose faith is deep and unquestioning may for that reason alone, receive the greatest benefits—an example of the faith referred to as the faith of little children. Doctors, psychiatrists and nurses know that patients who have mental reservations are less able to relax, to surrender, to accept, to realize with confidence that their essential need is the degree of receiving which demands surrender.

For we have to bring something; unless we bring the realistically positive co-operation we cannot hope to benefit; rather like listening to good music, our first contribution is the mind ready to surrender into receptivity.

As we thought and talked about all these things, eager to undertake anything likely to heal, we knew that whilst the desire to be healed was an indescribable yearning, it was in Dorfs' case a desire for the complete healing which is so much more than physical healing, the healing of the whole person. She knew, and I knew, that anything else would lack conviction; and that would mean insincerity. She would have interpreted it as an attempt to bring divine influence to bear on a purely physical condition, a subordinating of the whole to a part of it. Her faith in God precluded that.

Never were we in danger of forgetting our first-hand knowledge of the efficacy of Christian Science, of Spritiualism, of faith-healers. The diversity of the vehicles is ample evidence of the reciprocal need and responsibility—we have to be in harmony, not only completely but positively, with the vehicles and instruments and ways of healing which we sincerely believe to be *ours* in the sense of *our* being able and ready to co-operate in the fullest degree.

Confronted with this, Dorfs knew that she could not embark on anything which meant sacrificing her allegiance to medical science; whatever medical science could offer she would always accept, gratefully co-operating in the fullest degree. Subject to that, she would with no less gratitude co-operate fully with whatever kinds of help might be offered to her.

Her clear understanding of her personal responsibility was consistently related to the fulfilling *as a person and a whole person,* of her strange assignment. She knew that her task involved thinking positively, avoiding invalidism and the drift into self-pity; she was inflexibly resolved to ignore her frustrations and limitations. She knew, beyond all guessing, that this way of co-operating with God, the utmost she could offer, would enable her to achieve, by grace, whatever might be God's purpose for her. That sounds heroic. It was, but not in her own mind, for the depth of her humility protected her from all pietistic arrogance. Faith and loyalty to God are stumbling and uncertain in their progress, beset with doubts, tears, the weariness of the soul and the God-starved, impoverished, exhausted periods when vision is dim; this humility, permeating her whole being, became the keynote of her living, upholding her; out of fragmentation it produced unity, and harmony from the discord of daily battling. Humility, so stern in its discipline, changes personality. That, too, we came to know, as serenity emerged; no lessening of the high-hearted gaiety of spirit for which so many remember her, but the gaiety was a flowering of the serenity. There was a radiating; it was as if she had made one final and irrevocable decision when she realized the full meaning of the diagnosis and in all probability something like that transpired. Never did she deviate from it.

Her resolve to accept and carry through her assignment reinforced her desire, and not only her desire, but her magnificent struggle to defeat the disease. This involved no contradictions, conflicts or disunity in her thinking. Everything she had was mobilized in the physical battle. She was determined to win physically if faith and courage could win. This resolute fight, illumined by conviction, enabled her—despite the progress of the disease—to say, and say knowingly, "I am being healed." Which was true. Not the physical disease, but the whole person.

# IV

## MYSTERY

No science will ever replace myth, and a myth cannot be made out of any science. For it is not that "God" is a myth, but that myth is the revelation of a divine life in man.

CARL JUNG

"WHAT IS HEALING?" asks a doctor, and answering his own question, he offers this new definition: "Healing," he says, "is a satisfactory response to a crisis," and he continues, "crisis, including the crisis of sickness, is an opportunity for adjustment to a higher quality of life."[1]

We witnessed Dorfs' response to crisis. We watched how she used the "opportunity for adjustment to a higher quality of life." Accepting a mystery, she knew that the ultimate decision was out of her hands, despite faith and the mustering of all her resources. Most significant of all, she knew, with utter conviction, that *whatever happened*, all would be well. For us, it became no longer difficult to believe that crisis, calamity, catastrophe may not always be as evil as they seem to be. In ways understandable only long after they crash into our lives—and not always, even then—they seem sometimes to provide "opportunities," the rejecting or misusing leading to bitterness and misery, the accepting leading to radiance, peace of mind.

"At a time of catastrophe," says Berdyaev, the Russian philosopher, "a process of ascetic purification takes place, in the absence of which there can be no spiritual life."[2]

Catastrophe, then, presents us with an opportunity, and this is the theme of contemporary religious thinking; time now to discard the haunting nineteenth-century idea of associating catastrophe with doom, or still worse, with punishment ordained by the Almighty. "Calamity," wrote Wordsworth, "the chastisement of Heaven."

At the heart of the human situation lies mystery. Without it, man could not face his deepest tragedies, when logic and argument are meaningless and the human imagination is too limited to encompass the idea of a divine plan. How unintelligent, for the finite mind to imagine itself capable of assessing the infinite, so often imagined as a giant replica of the finite! What effrontery, to try to measure what we can never understand, or even visualize! Writes the President of India, a thinker esteemed as highly in the West as in the East: "The seers, whatever their religion, ask us to rise to the conception of a God above gods, who is beyond image and concept, who can be experienced but not known, who is the vitality of the human spirit. . . ."[3]

This is no new discovery. In a book written anonymously six hundred years ago—a book constantly appearing in new translations, the author says: "All rational beings, angels and men, possess two faculties, the power of knowing and the power of loving. To the first, to the intellect, God who made them is forever unknowable, but to the second, to love, he is completely knowable, and that by every separate individual. . . . This is the everlasting miracle. . . . To know it for one's self is endless bliss; its contrary is endless pain."[4]

That thought is reflected in a contemporary dictionary definition, which describes mystery as "religious truth divinely revealed, especially one beyond human reason."

Fearing mystery, because he fears the unknown, man comes to welcome it. Nature's terrifying power of destruction, through drought, tornado, volcanic eruptions and every other way of wrecking human planning, haunts every generation. The imploring and the beseeching of the unknown can become adoring, the welcoming of power beyond human power, so often discovered to be beneficent. "Our minds need mystery as our bodies need food: without it, no matter how great our grasp of science, our learning, our rational knowledge, we shall be starved; for there is in us a longing for infinity, for what is beyond the realm of reason. . . ."[5]

Mystery baffles the intellect, but not the human spirit. The disciplined spirit welcomes it because, unlike the intellect, it can admit the validity without comprehending, save through that "power of loving," the miracle of the realm of the spirit which can transmute mystery into serenity. In its very stillness, this serenity is potent; it has affinity with the trust of a child, who can accept from the heart, no anxieties, no questioning. And in this sphere, the questioning which to the intellect might appear to be merit and a nourishing, robs us of peace. In this sphere all the intellect's antics and acrobatics become a menace. Here lies the tragedy of the intellectuals who are honestly groping for a faith but incapable of rejecting the purely intellectual approach. Pascal still speaks with authority, based on revelation recorded in his personal experience: "The heart has its reasons, which reason does not understand." The sickness of humanity results in part from the discovery of succeeding generations that human self-sufficiency is a mirage.

In the tragedy of discovering this, man can discover his own immense capacity for love, unplumbed, until his own helplessness scares him. Then, he may in awe and in silence, fall into the arms of God. Spiritual apprehending becomes the heart's answer to man's yearning for certainty, the intruding intellect at last aware that it may partially invade, but never conquer. Writing towards the end of a long life, Carl Jung puts it like this: "A man . . . must sense that he lives in a world which in some respects is mysterious, that things happen and can be experienced which remain inexplicable; that not everything that happens can be anticipated. The unexpected and the incredible belong in this world. Only then is life whole."[6] Jung always wrote as a scientist, not as a philosopher or from the angle of religion.

Science sets us a pattern; it has to assume certain things which cannot be proved. This is its method of research and its way of progress. Science recognizes that there are some problems we shall probably never solve, due not to their complexity but to their nature. By its nature, eternity is beyond human comprehending. So is the divine. We can waste a lifetime in arguing about these things. The alternative, the way of assumptions, brings peace of mind, but it does not involve forsaking reason.

Mind and heart exploring in harmony are confronted with massive evidence of continuity of the universe and of so many manifestations of love beyond human love as to teach the honest seeker to be humble. In awe he may become aware not only of majesty but of kinship with it, being a part of the incalculable vastness of a universe which displays no evidence of finality. Its perennial renewals, phase by unpatterned phase, carry us with it beyond time. And humility can protect us from the futility of fruitless argument.

In its slow, weary march towards its own emancipation, the human soul passes through periods of great clarity, when singing and joy and enchantment make the pilgrimage seem less fearsome. At these times there is sometimes born a completely new sense of eternity; stretching to the limits of personality, we may become aware that there is a rhythm totally different from the rhythm of daily routine, an imperceptible but certain sharing of what we know to be timeless and ethereal. Being outside the intellectual sphere, this demands rejection of the mind and its mechanism; quiet and silence, kneeling, adoration, dedication, surrender which contributes to the silence, prayer being neither vocal nor mental, but at last a relationship, a receiving, these make up the atmosphere in which we can be what, by grace, we are becoming. Pilgrimage calls for faith, courage and grace far more than for intellectual comprehending. How subtle are the arguments which shut us out of heaven! "Steer clear of stupid arguments," wrote St. Paul, "they settle nothing and lead nowhere."[7]

Modern man, overwhelmed by the incalculable repercussions of his recent scientific conquests, appears to be relentlessly propelled farther and farther into the jungle of interminable argument, obsessionally urged to probing, some of it, but by no means all of it, sound and indispensable to progress. Distortion is inevitable. The penalty of combining the idolatry of wealth with lust for power is intoxication; even thirst for knowledge tends to be a focus on greater and greater acquisitiveness. Swollen with arrogance, man is too pre-occupied to sense the starving of his personality. History is a tale of man's pride redeemed by his distress, his stupidity culminating in his remorse, and it would be a denial of history to imagine that this costly process will be permanently changed as a result of a few generations losing their way.

Maybe, as has happened in earlier centuries, despair may be the road to recovery. Discovery that the wheel is again coming full circle, that knowledge alone can be a husk. Through the mystery of man's intuitive demand for mystery, he may strike the trail. The dethronement of mere knowledge could, who knows, lead to a quest for knowledge of ourselves. Mystery of mysteries, we may re-arrange our priorities; where, then, would gentleness come, and harmony and understanding and the toleration which gives meaning to neighbourliness and all the priceless rewards of emancipation from the slavery of our own choosing?

# V

## STANDING BACK

Sorrow re-marries us to God.
              DANTE

EARLY ONE JANUARY morning, floating into half-consciousness after sound sleep, Dorfs became aware that she was home. A robin's song, fluting in the mistiness of her waking, suddenly miracled the incredible: she *must* be home, because the hospital in which she had just spent five weeks was in an area far too congested for robins.

Christmas had loomed up as a bleak prospect, yet it had become an astonishing discovery. We had gained a completely new conception of giving, for everyone on the hospital staff was giving in such prodigal ways, giving time and presents and treats and surprises, giving and refusing to stop giving, all with a baffling joy which was somehow different from the effervescent seasonal spirit; the formula, the answer, the secret, of course, was love in its sacrificial manifestation. No one could receive, as we received, without a stabbing awareness of sacrifices of many kinds, a dedication of Christmas. For us, Christmas came that year to have new interpretations, never to be forgotten.

Within ten days—home; to our greatest adventure of all, seeming from the moment of the return to be coming into a new world. For time had already begun to mean something totally different from time as we knew it only a few weeks earlier.

Time splintered into fragments is robbed of its essence; its continuity withers. Without the wholeness of time, harmony becomes discord, which is its denial. Time whole and fragmented time are not related as one and part of one are related. Their nature differs. Out of the wholeness of time can come calm, contentment, poise, tranquillity; its splintering breeds restlessness.

Soon we came to understand something which so often is learned only because it is forced on us—that withdrawals can be a way into the wholeness of time. The rejecting, even the forced rejecting, of a broken rhythm is to regain a wholeness which is a largeness. Gradually, the largeness can become spaciousness. Vision widens. Perception becomes clearer, perspective truer. Shedding, we can gain; much that we shed we come to recognize as a destroyer. Less contriving; eventually great audacity in mental exploring, the imagination becoming more and more creative. In Bedford gaol, three hundred years ago, Bunyan, unaware that he was giving the world a masterpiece, a "best-seller" from its first publication to the present time, wrote *Pilgrim's Progress*. In Reading gaol Oscar Wilde, disillusioned by the tinsel brilliance of his own achievements, wrote his last prose work, recording what profound truths he had discovered in the long, forced withdrawal from the world:

"... the silence, the solitude, the shame—each and all of these things I had to transform into a spiritual experience.... Now I find hidden somewhere away in my nature something that tells me that nothing in the whole world is meaningless and suffering least of all. That something hidden away in my nature, like a treasure in a field, is humility. It is the last thing left in me, and the best ... of all things it is the strangest; one cannot give it away and another may not give it to one. One cannot acquire it except by surrendering everything that one has. It is only when one has lost all things, that one knows one possesses it ... he who can look at the loveliness of the world and share its sorrow, and realize something of the wonder of both, is in immediate contact with divine things, and has got as near to God's secret as anyone can get.... Where there is sorrow there is holy ground."[1]

This is an aspect of time which by its nature identifies it with eternity; using time wisely, man can come to live in a rhythm of harmony, deliberately discarding what splinters times, spurning the seductiveness of disharmony, cherishing and safeguarding

the fought-for serenity; discipline and perseverance and renunciation ultimately rewarded by conviction which is beyond all
uncertainty.

Time in this sense is measured by depth and intensity; duration
may be of no account. Its manifestations are infinitely diverse;
love at first sight and St. Paul's blinding conversion on the
Damascus road are only widely-varying examples of an alchemy
which can operate instantaneously. By the same alchemy comes
so much that is potent in contemplation. Monica Baldwin recounts
a conversation with the late Lord Dawson in which she referred to
"the power-houses of the great contemplative orders—Carthu-
sians, Cistercians, Carmelites, Benedictines and the rest—which,
by their hidden lives of prayer and penance supplied the necessary
spiritual force." "People who were united to God," she continues,
"were able, in virtue of that union, to do more for God in one
second than during a lifetime of merely human activity."[2]

Among so many tragedies of which men speak, seldom is
there mention of the killing of time; time frittered away, aimless,
meaningless, a sacrifice to nothingness; ineffectual sacrifice, for
no peace lies here.

Forced living in a backwater can have dramatic effects and
influences on your thinking. Indeed, the very character of your
thinking is changed. At first, perhaps, restlessness. We have
become accustomed to the fragmentation of the day. Difficult to
imagine how we shall be able to compass several hours of relative
inaction; the very idea is a reminder of our insatiable demand for
changes, even minor changes in the routine of the day. Apparently
this is a common experience among people who go into retreat,
the first day or so being often difficult; far more difficult, we are
told, is the experience of many who visit monasteries for more
than a brief stay. There is a sudden shock; the totally different
rhythm is neither gradual nor cushioned.

All these are inevitable preliminary reactions; time, varying
with mental approach as well as personality, is needed for
adjustment.

But there is a fundamental difference between backwater chosen for retreat, rest or replenishing and the backwater into which we can be forced by illness, uncertain as to duration and by its nature likely to demand inaction on a scale incalculable but beyond questioning. Of course, we tend to leave Mother Nature out of our calculations. Invalids often smile at the genuine astonishment of visitors who can hardly believe that despite restrictions and an apparently narrowing life, the days are not long enough. Not all invalids share this happy experience; not by any means. Loneliness among the sick is surely the most poignant loneliness in the whole world; visitors to hospitals know how magically it can for a while be dispelled by even a smile in passing; one of the tragedies of loneliness is our reluctance to believe how very easily it can be relieved.

They are indeed fortunate whose days prove not to be long enough, whose life, instead of narrowing, broadens as suffering enlarges sympathy, one horizon succeeding another until something approaching serenity pervades and permeates. This is something to which we can attain, not something occurring like quiet after noise; something battled for and won, no lessening of distress or pain or sorrow but the warrior's triumph.

This, Dorfs came to know, the battling and the near-defeat, the daily enduring, yet any initial speculation about how to compass prolonged inaction was subsequently difficult to recollect, so slight was its duration. Indeed, it can hardly be said to have had duration, for the adjustments seemed to be immediate, and so harmonious as to leave only the timeless time, which is the antithesis of boredom.

Re-thinking in this atmosphere tends to be less diffused because intrusions are fewer and on days when interruptions, those deadly destroyers of real thinking, are rare, clarity becomes possible. In backwater, the focus is changed. In forced backwater the prolongation of withdrawal from normal daily activities alters valuations so dramatically that it can become quite difficult, after a few months, to understand how one could ever have been interested in this or that feature in newspapers, radio, TV, or the social round. This is by no means a question of sour grapes, but it can be, and in our case it certainly was, a genuine feeling that we had become enriched by much of the apparent diminishing of our world, proving gradually to be its enlarging. The quality of quiet became deep enough to resent, more and more, its forced ending.

Surprisingly soon, we realized with heightening intensity, withdrawn from our normal rhythms and programmes of living, the destructive effects of the fragmentation of the day as it is lived by the great majority of people. How busy, how over-full the programme; nearly always too much to do, too many activities and intrusions on one's time. Social life added to business life, civic and community and a host of miscellaneous obligations, most of them seeming unavoidable, many desirable and some few we may not gladly forgo. In total, wearing, devitalizing; the wise balance between duties and hobbies almost impossible to maintain. Solitude and quiet and times with no programme at all, not only rare, but tending to be avoided because to stop suddenly, trying to rest when you are out of breath, relaxing when you are too taut to relax—these are difficult.

Come gently to quiet. At first it yields no rewards. They are elusive, fugitive, unpredictable. After apprenticeship we may surprise ourselves by new awareness of minute thrills—bird-song and the slant of sunlight, the heart of a daisy, the slope of a hill. None of this is the exclusive world of poets or philosophers. You find them so unexpectedly; then the fairies are beckoning. Catch the gossamer thread and follow it—in silence, or you may lose it. Fairies abominate noise. By halting you may have an exciting adventure in liberation, freeing yourself from trivialities, saving yourself by losing yourself.

For whatever reasons, each decade in this century has intensified the pace of living. Simplifying life by gadgetry is not always wise simplifying; sometimes the gadgets won't work and unless they are regularly serviced, the most important gadgets are useless.

Shorter working hours spotlight the real problem; instead of learning how to use the freedom from work we have demanded that radio, television, new forms of gambling and even more cosy vice shall always be available to fill in time. Odd that we complain of having no free time, yet refuse to have free time. We fill it in. Then we kill it. It has become too easy—the radio switch, the lift of the phone, the popping in. Time as opportunity becomes too naïve an idea; compelled to choose, the treadmill generations rarely choose time for solitude, because solitude is confused with solitariness, which is frightening until one discovers that solitude is healing, and discovers, far more importantly, that the frightening was fear of being alone. Emancipated from the tedium of so much now committed to machines, from unhealthy working conditions, long working hours, insecurity, poverty, man in the affluent society is bewildered, lacking direction.

Regal in a dominion only rarely invaded, many a sufferer from chronic or grave illness has in this sense built a new world. Never bored, never wanting time to hasten, luxuriating in its expanse, its timelessness, we could not be arrogant, surveying the hustle and restlessness as from a theatre, no longer on the stage but as spectators. Increasingly, we came to view the stage as a revolving stage.

If you are fortunate in sharing this, then not only are you aware of standing back, remote from the world's wrangling and clamour and the confusion of din; you are on a hill, invigorated by its clean air. Tuned to the rhythm of withdrawn quiet, you may become aware of the diminishing significance of your suffering. Long after she knew the full diagnosis and its implications, Dorfs said, "I wouldn't change places with anyone." As the range of your new interests widens, the intensity of real enjoyment becomes heightened. Has something in you been dormant, awaiting this strange awakening? Is the apparent limitation, the shrinking of opportunities a way into new zestful living? As you shut out more and more trivialities, you may wonder; so much now seems irrelevant as you focus on what you resolve to make into a full life. Your new remoteness challenges, and establishes new priorities; all that hinges on compassion acquires new relevance. "There is a curious freedom of mind and spirit and a new insight into the very nature of experience"[3] —this occurs in a letter from a young mother, severely paralysed and lying on her back for nearly ten years. It was in this spirit that Dorfs said, months after leaving hospital, "If I thought that they could find out more about the complaint to benefit someone else, I would go into hospital again."

Standing back, you may for the first time, and certainly in new ways, come to realize that you are no longer imprisoned by the world's concentration on its own sectional strivings and self-interest; now, they seem to emit smoke which hangs like a pall, blearing the eyes of all who have to shape the world, those who bear the responsibilites of government, so often seeming to guide it, not towards its destined goal but into one new respite and relief after another, their successive disillusionments forcing the caravanserai across to another and another part of the desert, deceived by its mirage, heedless of the compass needle pointing inevitably to the pole star. Outsoaring the earth-mists, not limited by your ordeal, nor yet in spite of it, but through it and because of it, you may be shielded by your forced stepping back, enabled to see, to perceive, to apprehend more clearly.

Politicians, expediency their impulse, cannot be expected to gaze at the pole star; the few who dare, become statesmen. Nor do the stars draw the mass of men, the driven millions crying for someone to lead them. Believing in action, they seldom know the stillness in which direction comes. Men are frightened of stillness; to miss the timeless gazing is for the majority no deprivation. A few prophets and poets, and those withdrawn, can now and then glimpse the stars and in humility envision some hardly trodden track which brings men nearer to them, across the centuries; their number is pathetically minute.

Among the withdrawn are the suffering—privileged, if they can avoid bitterness, to contribute more than they may realize, to the lighting of the path.

# VI

## CHALLENGE

Submission is a passive, negative thing that implies resignation and even resentment. But active, willing, conscious
acceptance of our share in the tragedy of life, this is something positive and creative. In turning such experience to
creative use we have first to understand the laws under which
these elemental things like pain operate. If you are prepared to
face pain in this way, accepting it and believing that it can be
turned to practical use, you make a strange discovery. Not
only do you find out the way to bear it so that it hurts you less;
you know that in its willing acceptance there lie ways of
growth in personality and sympathy and enrichment of life
which before you never suspected. There are few things more
inspiring than the sight of a great misfortune cheerfully and
heroically borne; and it is in the manner of its acceptance
that there lies the key. It is not the suffering but the way it is
borne which ennobles.

DR. J. L. WILSON, BISHOP OF BIRMINGHAM

T ODAY'S MOST POIGNANT questions are old questions;
"Why do innocent people suffer—and especially children?"
"How can there be a God of infinite power and love—if He
had the power, isn't it the first evidence of His love that He
would end suffering, stop wars, bring peace into the world . . .?"
And so on.

By men of all creeds and of none, these and similar questions
have been asked from one generation to another. Thousands of
sermons are preached, thousands of books have been written, on
various aspects of the mystery. No wonder we tend to become
confused. Suffering is evil, therefore, God being good, suffering
is the enemy of good and a denial of God. God's plan for us is
health, wholeness, holiness, all related to each other. Suffering,
disease, the absence of health, shows by its conquests that there is
no God. All so simple. And over-simplifying omits so many
aspects of suffering which can never be ignored by thoughtful
people, striving honestly to understand, even partially, the
diversity of problems related to suffering.

Time and again, we became aware of the need to remind
ourselves that some problems can never be solved. Philosophers,
scientists and statesmen recognize this, in trying to make any
theories and any scheme of life valid; *some problems can never be
solved.* In mundane affairs this identifies the thinker as mature; in
spiritual affairs (and suffering is an affair of the spirit) its recognition can be the way through, from near-despair towards
serenity. For the serenity notable among sufferers is so seldom
due to their tragic problems being solved. Coming to terms with
the problem implies some kind of faith; if it develops into conviction, peace ensues, peace which at its richest can become an

imperturbable core at the centre of one's being. It has to be fought and won, never as finality; it is a daily encounter. Dorfs found great inspiration in Brian Hession's experience, recorded so graphically in his book *Determined to Live*, which he wrote after the cancer operation which only one surgeon could be found to tackle; in letters, she quoted his phrase about "sweating it out with God, day by day," which had become imperative in winning her way through. Hession wrote:

"I think courage is not something that you put on at high moments of your life, but something that you have to sweat out alone with God, day by day. Suffering should be stepping-stones, not stumbling-blocks, and so I pray and battle with God for strength, for He says that His strength is made perfect in our weakness. I am a weak vessel for Him to fill."[1]

This idea of a vessel became paramount in Dorfs' interpretation of her assignment; she avoided discussion of any aspect of her ordeal. Brimful of life in its richest sense, she became increasingly aware of *being used*, as Hession knew himself to be used. "Whatever little I achieve," she wrote to a friend, "is due to influences known and unknown, to friends, also known and unknown, and to all-abiding love within this home. I am but the vehicle, receiving, transporting and in some small way endeavouring to deliver; a humbling experience."

Serenity can be personified in battle-scarred pilgrims, humility radiant, all sense of personal victory disowned. Claiming no longer to know why the burden of ordeal came, they emerge from the crucible with something which enables them to relegate their own sufferings to a fading memory. Epstein, who distilled the bitterness of a hostile world into rare beauty, bequeathing it as his creative response to hostility and suffering records this in his autobiography:

"O Sorrow, I have lived and wrestled with
you so long, and suddenly, seeing the beauty
of your face, I embrace you."

None of this implies a welcome to ordeal; human frailty limits
us at best to unrebellious, unembittered acceptance, but acceptance interpreted so co-operatively that triumph, through grace,
becomes possible.

If the river of healing is to make us whole, its bed may have
to be channelled deep and still deeper, to envelop us, until
anguish links us to the divine suffering, almost, but never completely, overwhelmed. This sharing helps us to identify ourselves
with the sufferings of others. Shared suffering changed the climate
of our social encounters during the last war: less froth, more
genuine friendliness, no less fun, but in addition to fun, funda-
mentals. In the crucible of war we were fired and cleansed;
thinking was clarified, there were many re-valuations, neighbourliness became real. Through fear we came to reverence, the
eternal pattern. It was not shameful to pray. Liberation deluded
us into the old self-swindle, man's belief, when ordeal ends, that
God is unnecessary and can be ignored. Apart from restlessness
and lack of purpose, the cost is represented by man's haunting
fear that at unprecedented speed, he is heading in the wrong
direction.

Suffering can sometimes provide the only conditions in which
an assignment can be carried out; love then becomes compassion-
ate, the giving which is completely self-forgetting; this can
energize. This kind of love is a healing thing, uniting, unifying,
making whole; it can banish pain, heal sickness, dispel despair.
It is the silver lining, the sun breaking through, and out of discord it can strangely bring harmony.

The drunkard wallowing in self-pity, and every other self-
indulgent sufferer, later wallowing in remorse, is by his own
stupidity prevented from sharing in any of this. Specifically, it
applies to tragic suffering, surrounded by mystery as deep as

history is long. When the challenge of this kind of suffering is accepted positively, it can result in a new attitude to living. Through acceptance, which demands a decisive choosing, the assignment can govern and condition everything in that positive way without which acceptance has no meaning. Handicaps and deprivations and infirmity can, through acceptance, become recognized as the *only* conditions in which the assignment—now regarded as a positive thing—could be fulfilled.

Maude Royden, famous preacher, and a Doctor of Divinity, who suffered physically for most of her life, said this when she was about seventy years old:

"The horrible thing about much of our suffering is that it seems so futile. What good does it do—this unchosen, undesired, stupid, useless pain?—It need not be futile: that is my comfort. It can be, and a thousand times it is, an inspiration. To whom do you turn when it is your turn to suffer? To one who suffers or has suffered—no one else can help you. You look for one who can prove to you in his own body that pain can be endured, that it can be conquered. If I want help in bearing pain, I find it in the hope that I am taking my share in the world's pain. I cannot choose it, not being very brave, but I can accept it in that way—endurance of pain is part of the price to be paid for lifting the world out of the jungle and the morass into which it has fallen—."[2]

The present Bishop of Birmingham, the Right Rev. J. L. Wilson, M.A., D.D., C.M.G., quoted in the extract which precedes the opening of this chapter, was Bishop of Singapore during the Second World War and was captured by the Japanese, imprisoned, tortured and subjected to terrible privations. After the war he returned to prepare and confirm his jailers in the Christian faith.

In these conditions of real fulfilment, dedication follows discipline, the discipline making the dedication more fruitful.

Suffering can in this way become a road to serenity; this we were to discover and to prove by arduous experience. Often it was an exhausting climb. Hazards were not always recognized as hazards; they might have terrified us, if not, indeed, defeated us. Mercifully, the future is veiled. Between one day's battling and the next, we seemed to be replenished and equipped to stride ahead into ever uncharted country and the growing awareness of this was a gentling and mellowing and healing, making the way ahead a little less bleak, less sombre, less threatening. Twenty-four hours seems to be the divine assessment of man's capacity for carrying his burden and if we are wise, we use the dark hours for the replenishing, through that more complete surrender in which oblivion can become sleep.

Stumbling forward from one day's problems into the next, known beforehand to present new complexities due to progressive muscular decline, we came to realize that there was frequently new clarity, and a beckoning instead of a baffling. So striking and so varied were these reactions; they could change the day. The fearsome often became the feasible. Longing to come through the day well became a hope, hope merged into a realization that this day was somehow being managed. In the day's retrospect, many an evening underlined its tranquillity, tranquillity not as immunity from something, or as an escape, but a pervading peace through and during the battling, helping us to face more confidently whatever might be our tomorrow.

Because Dorfs had faced the worst, the worst as it insidiously invaded was utterly incapable of defeating her. This disease is unpredictable in its course. What a patient can do one day may next day be impossible; which muscles, which limb might be affected—she was given neither direction nor warning. That sinister realization led to a philosophy which served her well; she referred to it as "daily bread." Imagination is not strained in picturing the progressive limitation due to a deteriorating muscular condition. But she convinced herself and all of us that she would be given both the strength and the guidance to tackle each day's problems as they came along. From this emerged a simple rule (oh, that the world might use it!) "trying to solve tomorrow's problems today doesn't work." Spotlighted through her personal experience came the recognition that until we are actually in tomorrow, the conditions in which tomorrow's problems can be wisely solved do not exist.

And could there be a lovelier mystery than this, that out of suffering can be distilled a quality and perfection of peace quite beyond describing? This is eternal mystery, the quest of the ages, all the accumulated wisdom of man proving utterly incapable of discovering, in the earthly sense, even a clue. In the unearthly sense, intellect barred, the answer is so simple as to demand only the innate wisdom of a child. Nor is this experience reserved for so-called "religious people." It is for the lost as well. For all who are adrift, not something they are expected to achieve, but something calling for surrender. Peace of mind is by no means reserved for those called on to face catastrophe or the long endurance of ordeal, yet these are apparently the only, the inevitable ways for many people; many have been assigned to ordeal so completely beyond their capacity to endure that only surrender into "outside resources" quite inexhaustible, could crown them with radiance. Radiating peace, light, harmony, they bring us no reminder of their ordeal. The perfume of a rose is to be enjoyed, no reminder of the nitrogen, the clay and the winter, without which roses do not flourish; the indefinable radiance of many sufferers is their rose.

The limitations of the isolated sufferer, withdrawn and stranded in backwater, may, then, be only apparent. They may be essential, indispensable. Without them, attainment may be impossible; not achievement, which implies action, but the infinitely more difficult inaction, and the surrender, surrender into the illimitable, convincing us that once we avail ourselves of what is beyond assessing and beyond all our needs, our resources are adequate.

Attainment through this kind of surrender is an overcoming; there is no higher manifestation of the human spirit's ability to conquer, a conquering through a surrendering. The attainment can outshine whatever achievement might have been won through stern resolve alone. It is inspirational; the unquestioning obedience, the faith which is "belief when we cannot see." Radiance which is potent indeed becomes pervading, an unmistakable transmission of energy. For many sufferers undoubtedly become,—through their suffering—messengers, channels through which power mysteriously passes.

Out of turmoil can come not only calm, but new direction. As the coats of veneer which protect us from society gradually peel off—society being almost forsaken—the real person, no longer smothered, gradually emerges towards destined fulfilment. Instead of nightmare, suffering can be night preceding dawn. Darkness is not only inevitable; it is part of the eternal process. And there is a sense in which suffering is a state of darkness. Part of the mystery is that some of us have to go through periods of darkness in which struggle and aspirations and all our efforts towards faith seem to result in frustration. For our progress, apparent failure seems to be as essential as success. Times when God seems inaccessible can be the hammering of the gold. "I have never found anyone," wrote Thomas à Kempis, "however religious and devout, who did not sometimes experience withdrawal of grace—when the spirit of devotion is aflame in your heart, you should consider how you will fare when the light leaves you. When this happens, remember that this light will one day return, which I have now for a while withdrawn——"[3]

Even more significant than the arid and dark periods are our apparent failures. Nothing tests faith more than failure, yet without it, the divine purposes cannot be fulfilled and in that sense, some, at any rate, of our failures contribute to success—the ultimate success beyond human visualizing. Interviewed before he left York to become Archibishop of Canterbury, Dr. Michael Ramsey said ". . . we are here as a Church to represent Christ crucified before the world. And because that is so it may be the will of God that our Church should have its heart broken and perhaps the heart of the Archbishop broken with it, just because we are here to represent Christ and Christ's compassion. But if that were to happen it wouldn't mean that we were heading for the world's misery, but quite likely pointing the way to the deepest joy."

So defeat and apparent failure may be the way, even the only way, to real victory. It is the story of Calvary, history's most terrifying defeat, without which history's most triumphant victory could never have been. It is the story of Gethsemane, when ALL the disciples fled. The story comes down the ages, from saints and martyrs to simple, suffering folk; this is the mystery of defeat transmuted into victory. So easily we forget it. In ordeal, more, perhaps, than in any other way, we come to learn that our real needs are—in mysterious ways—always cared for, not always in what we have imagined to be the best ways. Even evil can be used to contribute to ultimate good; our responsibility is to deal with evil in the right way in the encounters from which no one escapes. Suffering has led men out of their misery and restlessness to the most inspiring of all discoveries, the discovery of the real self.

Challenge evokes courage, "the virtue which makes all other virtues possible." Courage to respond to the decisive challenge of tragedy has the compelling force of crusading; it is infectious and splendid, sweeping away the petty and the irrelevant, an emancipating experience. Before we are born, challenge is in us; without it, no baby would struggle into a new world. It is fight for survival, the abandonment of inertia; it dares to envision, to dream, to explore, to plan and to build. It is an upsurging, a dedicated, relentless drive out of chaos into direction and resolve and into believing, the believing which is strengthened by discipline and by enduring.

Challenge born out of catastrophe leads to a disillusioning and a discarding; discarding all preoccupation with ourselves, we emerge ready to give and to serve in new ways. "Tragedy," wrote Dr. W. E. Sangster, himself a victim of progressive muscular atrophy, "is often fruitful of good. Lighthouses are

built by drowned sailors. Roads are widened by mangled motor-
ists. Frustration and testing have had a major part in the higher
triumphs of our race."

Which spotlights the patient research, the progress in conquering disease, raising standards of health, improving physical
fitness, extending the span of life and easing pain; to all this,
sufferers have contributed the essentials. Without them, research
would have little to record. Suffering for others is fortunately a
deep response in man's make-up. History would be a poor tale
without that kind of suffering. It is the mother giving, sacrificing,
and suffering, for her child. Every family has proof of it. It changes
"Why should it happen to me?" into "Why shouldn't it happen
to me?" And whilst the mystery remains, the ministry of suffering
can become a healing.

If we think of the human body as a family it is easy to visualize
one member suffering for the wellbeing of the family. Nature
finds many ways of calling attention to a sick body; the throat
or the foot or any other member may be selected to suffer, often
resulting in healing of far more than the particular member.
Nor should we forget that so much physical suffering is preventable. If we flout the laws of health, why blame God? Over-eating,
heavy drinking and many other abuses and indulgences have
ultimately to be paid for. Violating Nature's laws accounts for a
host of illnesses; in an age of tension, fear, insecurity and disharmony, they become more sinister, involving mental break-
downs and emotional stresses which widen a vicious circle.
Common sense demands that preventable suffering should be
recognized for what it is and subjected to the disciplines which
can lead to harmony, healing, wholeness. There remains the
insoluble mystery of suffering, which forces every sufferer to
make a decision.

Suffering is a challenge. Brought to the Cross, it is a rich
offering, a very sharing of the Cross, mystery to mystery; as we
kneel, wordless and waiting, patient, receptive, the consciousness
of pain assuaged can become real; the tortured soul can be

c

calmed, shedding its stress and all striving, then, imperceptibly, there can be an indefinable replenishing, grace and courage for the day.

Only by our deliberate choosing can this way open. An assignment accepted co-operatively brings awareness of unknowable outside resources. Now we come to prove by experience, sure beyond all doubting; never again need we puzzle to define, to explain or to understand. In the utterness of the overwhelming, far out beyond our depth, surrender has become neither chaos nor defeat, but conviction about reality; at last we can come to realize that being a part of God, we are invincible so long as we are loyal.

The triumph is the healing of the whole person. None but the saints can welcome suffering, but thousands have found seeming defeat to be a beginning instead of an ending. We shall not escape pain and suffering, but "escape at all costs" can be replaced by the discovery that pain and suffering may be a way, not of escape, but infinitely better, a way through; a way into the long road which can lead to triumph over fear.

Triumph over fear is replacement of dominant fear by dominant harmony. Courage alone cannot ensure this triumph; it calls for more than virtue and more than the human will can mobilize. Stern resolve is not enough, nor the discipline that tempers it. Allegiance to something outside ourselves has to challenge all that draws us, heart and mind alike, towards ourselves, because focus on ourselves is the road to self-pity. In ordeal the shift of focus away from ourselves is rarely attainable unless something compelling, something splendid and vibrant replaces the ego. This is a crisis in human devotion. Give yourself to something beyond your achieving, something unlikely to bring personal rewards, this is the replacement of the ego and its defeat. Whatever is a dedication leads towards triumph because dedication means a forgetting of the ego.

In any age, only the few are dedicated. For the vast majority of us, hope lies in worship and we hesitate and hold back; for worship is unreal unless it is supreme and selfless devotion. Supreme and selfless devotion is a continuing sacrifice; it is an affair of blaze and fervour as well as loyalty, impossible for faltering humanity to maintain in relation to anything less than the divine.

Along this road, selfless love can triumph over fear. Out of ordeal, radiance; battle-scars no longer signposts to despair, but symbols of the triumph.

# VII

## ABOVE ALL THINGS

Religion will not regain its old power until it can face change in the same spirit as does science. Its principles may be eternal, but the expression of these principles requires continual development.

A. N. WHITEHEAD

CRISIS, WHEN IT affects life and death, compels you to think about religion; to think differently, for your world has changed. You may think about it with contempt, convinced of its irrelevance, all right for fuddy-duddies, but outworn as a force. Or, like Dorfs, you may find that its dynamic sets something ablaze in you. Always, her religion had been deep and real, governing her living; what emerged from the ordeal is well-expressed by a comment made by her doctor about a year after her hospital tests—"She has saintliness," he said, "and it inspires me immensely." Saintliness is not sainthood; it is a quality which can be developed, becoming part of character. We tend to become like whatever we associate with, good or evil, lovely or despicable. When suffering leads to selflessness, saintliness may develop. Good can then come out of evil; even when Calvary daunts you, you will be upheld. Through terrifying experience you can come to know instead of believing; no more guessing, doubting, wondering, theorizing. With conviction, and quite calmly, you can re-arrange your priorities, re-organize your life, the completeness of faith replacing all the uncertainties that haunt most of us, for most of our lives.

Not even this conviction will prevent your wavering; the battles are daily battles and you will still be human, losing some and winning others. But ultimate triumph can be yours. All through the ages, distress has brought man to God. There is a kind of tidal motion. When things go well, we tend to ignore God; when they go wrong, we implore and beseech and beg for relief and release. In our solitariness we come, lonely and surrendering; so often the prodigal returns only when he is at the end of his tether.

Human bewilderment and heartbreak and inconsolable loneliness often reveal man as depending on the self he secretly distrusts. With no one to love in any sacrificial sense, his self-love consuming his desire for love, fear envelops him like a fog; direction lost, he is brought face to face with his own hopelessness. Searching for peace in imagined freedom, the undisciplined heart robs itself of liberty; its pseudo-liberty is not even licence, which implies something allowed. The unlicence of the rebelling heart, uncommitted and acknowledging no loyalties, is a self-expelling; the outcast has separated himself from what he yearns for, what he is starving for—love which will forsake self. When that forsaking becomes a finding, he is on the road to peace, to the God he needs —and the God who needs him, for God, like man, needs to be needed. Keats has a phrase, "yearning like a God in pain."[1] In his extremity, man sometimes becomes aware of a beckoning; then the prodigal's urge sets him homeward.

You don't need to be a returning prodigal to learn that it is precisely at the end of your tether, and not until then, that the vitality of your religion determines the ordering of your life. We soon realized that we were hopelessly out of our depth. Then and not until then, we were swept into recognition of the unimportance of our own resources. With the recognition came the awareness of a new obligation. We had to co-operate. In the New Testament story, Jesus told the disciples who had caught nothing during a night's fishing to go out again and cast the nets on the other side of the ship; more arduous toil, no easy miracle but strain imposed on strain. This is the pattern; to the limit of endurance and seemingly beyond it, your assignment will compel you to keep on. "Endurance," wrote a friend, a few months before Dorfs died, "is a country beyond the known frontier— the place we go on to when we think we are through."

In your pilgrimage and your enduring, failures can sometimes nourish and energize you as no success can nourish you; always you are climbing, and climbing towards new horizons makes humility more real, because it dethrones the ego, the enemy of true religion. For religion is not essentially an affair of creeds or church-going. It is an affair of love. Creeds help many of us. To some they become crutches and to others chains. As means towards ends they can sustain and remind and guide; as ends, they hide us from God. As one friend wrote:

> "Apart from feeling the need of an anchorage in one or other of the churches, to help to weather the storms, more and more it seems that all the differences, dogmas, apostolic successions, methods of government, orders of service, matter less and less—in the end, the things that really *are* essential for this frantic world are just love and compassion, beauty and tranquillity."

From the Rector of the famous Bow Church in Cheapside, London, comes confirmation of this—"We should by-pass the dogmatic mind," he writes, "and study afresh the implications of the mind of love in the universe."[2]

Jesus left no creed beyond that contained in his two commandments:

> "Thou shalt love the Lord thy God with all thy heart, and with all thy soul and with all thy strength and with all thy mind; and thy neighbour as thyself."[3]

How can we love people whom we do not even like? "We think of some people we know," writes F. J. Sheed, "the man next door, perhaps, or the man we work under, and we do not find them in the least attractive. We would run a mile to avoid them. Does this mean that we have broken down on Christ's rule? Not at all. Loving people may *result* in our finding them pleasing to us; but that is not what it *means*. *To love someone means to want with the whole power of your will, what is good for that person.*"[4]

For the humble searcher, uncertain about dogma and creeds, one of the sure guides, distilled into less than fifty words, can be found in the English Prayer Book, but its ageless wisdom is hidden from the casual reader. The penetrating focus of the persevering student will reveal treasure; if he digs deep enough, not only thinking, but often meditating, he may even discover here a pattern for living. Here it is, the Collect for the Sixth Sunday after Trinity:

"O God, who hast prepared for them that love thee, such good things as pass man's understanding; pour into our hearts such love toward thee, that we, loving thee above all things, may obtain thy promises, which exceed all that we can desire; through Jesus Christ our Lord."

Three words stand out, as if to assess the measure of our loyalty to this love, "*above all things.*"

To love God means to worship Him. Worship in the sense of adoration of something unimaginably more beautiful, more powerful than man and all his wonders, capacities and achievements, something infinite, inspiring awe. There are yearnings which defy all human defining. They find their expression in worship, most of all in silent worship, the stillness, the emptying of the self which makes room for God. And we must make room voluntarily; God will not push the door open—"Behold, I stand at the door and knock." Even God can be heartbroken, knocking, waiting, listening, precluded from coming in because we are endowed with free-will, able to invite, able to refuse. No room without a renouncing; something we cherish has to go if it blocks the way. Until the barricades are down we cannot even be sure we hear the knock at the door. It seems as if there are so many times when God can do nothing for us until we fail. Utter helplessness can in some strange way be essential. Failure can so often be the only road to success, the prelude to that unreserved surrender which opens the way. For God will not share loyalty.

It is in this sense that man's urge for transcendence, for escape into something beyond himself, becomes compelling, for religion is instinctive; it is ineradicable, something which can temporarily be stifled, suffocated, denied, but never since the dawn of history has it been exterminated. Even in the stifling and the denying, something is at work, and most of all in our loneliness, in despair, which can be the road to hope through the realizing of a need for help beyond human help. Compassion then comes to have meaning; in the yielding, the masks fall off, the armour of resisting courage is discarded.

Twentieth-century man's deep longing for compassion is intensified because he has lost his way. He has lost it for identifiable reasons, at least two being of paramount importance. The first is that world war, previously unknown, deeply disturbed his rhythm of living, undermined his faith, distorted his sense of values and severely shook his morals; his self-esteem is at a low ebb. The second reason is that the church, to which he looked for guidance, has failed to discover and adopt new wave-lengths, adhering to many outworn forms as if forgetting that whilst its message is eternal, succeeding generations can receive it only on the changing wave-lengths which deafen the ear to so much that was so vital to their predecessors.

". . . there is no slackening of interest in vital religion, in a religion of life . . . the Churches do not 'speak to the condition' of the time. They are organized and equipped for a different generation than the one that happens just now to be here . . . the Churches are bound to face, in a more adequate way than has yet been done, the intellectual re-interpretation of the universe . . . people everywhere, especially young people, are confused in their thought of God. . . . They have little guidance and help. The old-fashioned answers and evidences do not convince. The problems are new ones. . . . The young seekers want honest, sincere guides who understand the issues, who have travelled through the fog and the shadows and who have come out on the hill-top into the light."[5]

Rufus Jones, a Quaker, wrote this. It is relevant to quote Dean

Inge: "The Quakers, of all Christian bodies, have remained nearest to the teaching and example of Christ."[6]

On this subject, President Masaryk wrote:

"The Church today and tomorrow will be more individual; it will answer the personal spiritual needs of people—I am not a prophet, but I think I am one of those future believers. We need freedom of science and research, intellectual integrity in matters of religion, we need tolerance too, but not spiritual indifference; no, what we need is faith, living faith in something higher than ourselves, something great, sublime, eternal."[7]

All this finds confirmation in a pronouncement by the Archbishop of Canterbury:

"Since the war our Church has been too inclined to be concerned with the organizing of its own life, perhaps assuming too easily that the faith may be taken for granted and needs only to be stated and commended. But we state and commend the faith only in so far as we go out and put ourselves with loving sympathy inside the doubts of the doubting, the questions of the questioners, and the loneliness of those who have lost their way."[8]

These quotations refer to the recoil from "churchianity," stressing the vitality of Christianity. When the church loses its dynamic it loses its significance and man wanders, adrift, until some kind of rebellion enables the church to re-discover its direction through re-alignment with God. In the fourteenth-century Christianity passed through a crisis so fundamental that when it emerged, re-vitalized, it was an emancipated, formative, dynamic influence instead of being inert and confused. When John Wesley set England on fire two hundred years ago, a stoned prophet, persecuted and maligned by the church of his fathers, he was battling against clericalism which had lost its vision. Ours is by no means the only epoch compelled to grope its way out of irreligion, and it is relevant to remind ourselves of what the earliest Christians had to face. In his preface to *Letters to Young Churches* J. B. Phillips summarizes:

". . . these letters were written, and the lives they indicate were led against a background of paganism. There were no churches, no Sundays, no books about the Faith. Slavery, sexual immorality, cruelty, callousness to human suffering, and a low standard of public opinion, were universal; travelling and communications were chancy and perilous; most people were illiterate. Many Christians today talk about the 'difficulties of our times' as though we should have to wait for better ones before the Christian religion can take root. It is heartening to remember that this faith took root and flourished amazingly in conditions that would have killed anything less vital in a matter of weeks. These early Christians were on fire with the conviction that they had become, through Christ, literally sons of God; they were pioneers of a new humanity, founders of a new Kingdom. They still speak to us across the centuries. Perhaps if we believed what they believed, we might achieve what they achieved."

Mounting evidence of a new upsurge within the churches may accelerate the overcoming of that weakness conspicuous in nineteenth-century religion in which denominationalism was dominated by political aspects, facing no challenge of revolutionary crises such as have confronted recent generations. Nineteenth-century industrialists found it congenial to support a church which hardly ever impinged on their nefarious acquisitiveness and in which a relatively uncritical, ill-formed population found solace.

Today's unscrupulous race towards prosperity, involving the sacrifice of standards of morality, and violation of so much that economic man counts as irrelevant,—all this has transformed the scene. God is counted as irrelevant by more people than would unashamedly assert this, and it seems necessary to discover the century's possible ways of even imagining what He is, and what He is like. This presents the churches with a major problem which, fortunately, they are beginning to study. God as a benevolent, bearded old gentleman living in the sky is gradually becoming no God for the new generations; all this was appropriate for ancient tribes trudging across endless waste lands, always open to the stars, accustomed to the notion of earth surrounded by sky, sky being God's home. For them God lived. Clinging to obsolete concepts of God, twentieth-century man has lost any idea of how to relate Him to the context of contemporary living. This is not the cause of the idolatry of wealth, the current "golden calf," but the idolatry has tragically coincided with man's separation from God, from anything virile in his thinking which could remind him of a *living* God. Fortunately, we are witnessing explosions of irreverence and scepticism which are disposing of much mental clutter. Explosions are uncomfortable, but if dynamite can make us dynamic, it is invaluable.

From a seat on the side-lines, well back from the arena, you may discern the early signs of something in this rebellion which inspired leadership can canalize into constructive channels, leading the new generations out of hideous despair, satisfying their inarticulate longing to be used for something worth living for as well as worth dying for. Scepticism is so often a rich breeding-ground; many a saint has come out of it, painfully but triumphantly. Restlessness itself is an activity, better than apathy, and the restlessness of the younger generations in particular has much wholesomeness. Below the self-indulgence there are unrecognized longings for liberation from bored satiety. Alienated and distrustful of themselves, they need evidence of validity before trusting anyone else and the only proof of validity in religion is sacrificial love. Information and instruction are part of the way out of confusion, but without sacrificial love they can be harmful as dust in the eyes of the seeker, a deterrent to progress when spiritual starvation cries out for the only effective nourishment. Later, when the challenging mind is disillusioned and freed from sordidness, when fear begins to be transmuted into friendliness and compassion opens the way into exaltation—then new worlds open. Through the proved selflessness of sacrificial love, God, imagined as obsolete, can become alive, the beginning of worthwhile living. Trivialities can then become recognized for what they are, direction and meaning can gradually emerge; at last, time can be filled instead of being killed. Instead of escape, or a way out, a way through can become more and more clearly discernible.

Only glimmerings? Maybe. But the yeast is working. In new ways, all too lamely acknowledged, the layman is becoming more intimately integrated as an active part of the church, no longer able to ignore his specific responsibilities. The nature of the responsibilities is changing. Traditionally there was parson in pulpit, sermon on Sunday and a secular week for all but a few; entirely new functions for both parson and pew are emerging as a new pattern. The pioneering of worker priests, industrial chaplains, and the part-time chaplains who also work in factories; services in homes, discussion groups, prayer groups and so many other new activities which are proving effective—these are perhaps the prelude to root and branch reorganization for which there are heartening signs of welcome within the churches.

Such initial changes—they are only beginnings—significantly encourage corporate worship, which is so vitalizing and so necessary, for the great majority of people. The few who more easily find spiritual replenishing in solitude, so completely different from solitariness, and the mystics—they will find their way. Those who are stranded in sick rooms and hospitals, in an atmosphere of the sacrificial love which symbolizes God, they, too, can find their way. We came to a rich realization of that; an awareness that neither deprivation nor disease can rob us of serenity. In long periods of quiet which were never long enough, we seemed to come to a perfect understanding of what religion is about, that it is concerned with the kind of love which can truthfully be called sacrificial. This was to Dorfs the essence of religion. Even after she knew the full diagnosis and its implications

she insistently held to this—"It is better to love than to be loved."
The love had come through a process of refining and trans-
figuring. Nothing to do with liking people, which implies
approval, but love for the loveless and the unlovable, the love
which is compassion and a deep sharing and this, after all, was
love as taught by Jesus, who was filled with love for prostitutes
and drunks and all who had been overwhelmed by sin, which is
separation from God, self-banishment, an estrangement and
consequently a state of unease.

Spiritual love is energizing, adding always to vitality. It is an
un-selfing, an activity of God, of whom we are part, made in His
image. We cannot visualize God but we can contemplate love
and we can live it. If this were an intellectual process there would
be no hope for the illiterate. "It is a humbling reflection," writes
Alan Richardson, Dean of York, "that after all one's years of
toil and study, one does not necessarily know the truth better
than a simple shepherd or a child."[9] The intellect can hinder full
recognition of divine love because it persists in trying to understand, and no one can understand divine love, which is concerned
with the heart, not the intellect. Had we been expected to understand, the human mind would have been totally different from
the apparatus which it is, even after centuries of training. It is
not less adequate than the human heart, but functionally different.
We cannot understand, but we can adore. Adoring, we achieve
harmony. This is an individual relationship between man and
God, the essential which is outside membership of any church,
allegiance to any creed.

"I asked one of the monks," writes Patrick Leigh-Fermor,
visiting a French monastery, "how he could sum up, in a couple
of words, his way of life. He paused a moment and said, 'Have
you ever been in love?' I said, 'Yes.' A large Fernandel smile
spread across his face. 'Eh bien,' he said, 'c'est exactement
pareil. . . . ' "[10] This kind of love is a commitment, supreme, the
governing and directing force in one's life—that or nothing.

*Religion is sacrificial love, translated into living.*

# VIII

## GATEWAYS

More things are wrought by prayer than this world dreams of.

Tennyson

ERIL DRIVES MAN to his knees. Not necessarily believing there is a God to pray to; it may be the depth of his despair being itself a blind hope. A cry in the wilderness. How rarely this word "wilderness" is used, and how vividly it conveys the idea of being completely lost, all sense of direction gone. In a sinking ship or a tumbling plane, when men are adrift, stranded, overwhelmed, they find it easy to pray. It is instinctive. "'O God,' I cried, and that was all." The parson who wrote that made it clear that merit counts for nothing—"That man is perfect in faith who can come to God in the utter dearth of his feelings and desires, without a glow or an aspiration, with the weight of low thoughts, failures, neglects and wandering forgetfulness, and say to Him, 'Thou art my refuge.'"[1]

The despairing cry is in itself relief, yet the distress may continue, the crisis may become calamity. Were it otherwise, prayer would be a glorified penny-in-the-slot machine, and among the things that prayer is not, this should perhaps be the easiest to understand. There is no magic. Prayer is so often answered in ways we don't interpret as answers, in ways we don't like, answered by refusals, by apparent ignoring, apparently not answered at all. Since even the saints confirm this, over and over again, their evidence can be accepted. They may have been asking for the wrong things, or for the right things at the wrong time. Answers can be misinterpreted. For our own good, the answers may appear to be diametrically opposite to what we asked for. This is recorded of Jesus. In Gethsemane, He had prayed that the cup might pass from Him. But He had to go to Calvary. The prayer in Gethsemane includes words which remove all ambiguities about what we can expect to receive—"*nevertheless, not as I will, but as Thou wilt.*"

To pray for the divine will to be done is true acceptance. The suffering may continue, but because our attitude towards it has *fundamentally* changed, we can find ourselves—the sufferers—standing, as it were, outside ourselves, partners in the divine purpose, the unrevealed purpose, all contained in a realistic conception of faith, maybe increased, maybe for the first time established and become potent as a sustaining influence; not any magic solution of grave problems, but the change of attitude in ourselves which, through acceptance, robs suffering of the stings of resentment, so violent, so corrosive, poisonous even, as we so insistently clamour for our own way.

The escapist, praying, finds no satisfaction. Satisfaction without surrender is impossible and surrender demands the renunciation which is "making room" for the divine will to operate. For in prayer there must always be an element of mystery. Generations accustomed to a routine of tabloid medicines learn this slowly; instead of pain, pill, peace, there is so often prolonged waiting, near-exhaustion, the testing of faith and apparent failure. No human formula has meaning here; if it had, we should be assessing divine power and plan in terms of human techniques and limitations, of our ways instead of the inscrutable ways. This need for surrender is probably a main cause of misunderstanding about prayer, what it is, what it can mean.

Poignantly, widespread ignorance is coupled with widespread yearning. Thousands would like to pray, but do not know how. Between the church and the bookshop the sincere enquirer can today find every form of guidance; one of his primary needs is to treat prayer as something to be studied, learned, practised, with serious application and perseverance such as we give to the study of anything in which we hope to achieve reasonable proficiency. Slovenly and casual approaches are as inffective in prayer as in any other activity.

Today's heartening emphasis on seven-day religion makes it easier to regard prayer not as the occasional parrot-like mumbling of a few sentences, but as yeast in the dough. In strange ways its yeastiness can become recognized. Helen Hayes, the famous American actress, tells how she learnt about prayer:

"Life seems to be a series of crises that have to be faced. In summoning strength to face them, though, I once fooled myself into an exaggerated regard of my own importance. I felt very independent. I was only distantly aware of other people. I worked hard and was 'successful.' In the theatre, I was brought up in the tradition of service. . . . But somehow the *meaning* of things escaped me.

"When my daughter died of polio everybody stretched out a hand to help me, but at first I couldn't seem to bear the touch of anything, even the love of friends; no support seemed strong enough.

"While Mary was still sick, I used to go early in the morning to a little church near the hospital to pray. There the working people came quietly to worship. I had been careless with my religion, I had rather cut God out of my life, and I didn't have the nerve at the time to ask Him to make my daughter well—I only asked Him to help me understand, to let me come in and reach Him. I prayed there every morning and I kept looking for a revelation, but nothing happened.

"And then, much later, I discovered that it *had* happened, right there in the church. I could recall, vividly, one by one, the people I had seen there—the solemn labourers with tired looks, the old women with gnarled hands. Life had knocked them around, but for a brief moment they were being refreshed by an ennobling experience. It seemed as they prayed their worn faces lighted up and they became the very vessels of God. Here was my revelation. Suddenly I realized I was one of them. In my need I gained strength from the knowledge that they too had needs, and I felt an interdependence with them. I experienced a flood of compassion for people. I was learning the meaning of 'Love thy neighbour'. . . ."[2]

Helen Hayes says she was "only distantly aware of other people"—all transformed when prayer became a force in her daily living, and here is equally interesting but totally different evidence from one of the greatest social investigators, Beatrice Webb:

"A secularist friend once cross-examined me as to what exactly I meant by prayer; he challenged me to define the process of prayer, to describe its happening. I answered that I would gladly do so if I could find the words. The trouble is, as Tagore observed about poetry, that words have meanings, or, as I should prefer to say, *predominantly intellectual meanings*; and that in prayer, even more than in poetry, it is emotion and not reason that seeks transmission. Religion is love; in no case is it logic. That is why, down all the ages of human development, prayer has been intimately associated, whether as a cause or as an effect, with the nobler and more enduring forms of architecture and music; associated, too, with poetry and painting, with the awe-inspiring aspects of Nature, with the great emotional mysteries of maternity, mating and death. In another place I may try (and probably fail) to express, by the clumsy mechanism of the written word, the faith I hold; that it is by prayer, by communion with an all-pervading spiritual force, that the soul of man discovers the purpose or goal of human endeavour, as distinguished from the means or process by which human beings may attain their ends."[3]

Beatrice Webb's phrase "communion with an all-pervading spiritual force" confirms the idea of surrender to the divine will and helps in finding the answer to a question so frequently asked, and so understandably—why, if God exists, if He is loving as well as powerful, we are expected to pray at all. And since we can add nothing to God's power, of what use is human prayer? Only one answer has been found. God's way of running the world demands our co-operation. Whatever His reasons may be, the evidence is clear; when we refuse to co-operate, His plan for us is distorted, is deprived of maximum fulfilment. This is the burden and responsibility of free-will. History records man's co-operation alternating with his efforts at self-sufficiency, his periods of peace of mind alternating with periods of distress, the prodigal's self-loathing and his trudge home, asking to be received on his father's terms, *whatever they may be.*

Yet this is only one aspect of a many-sided subject. Prayer is so much more than a cry in distress. More than all our cries, more than "talking to God," which is so general as the notion of what prayer is—a perfectly understandable notion, since prayer is associated with corporate worship, with services of so many kinds, on TV and radio as well as in churches, associated too with "days of prayer," prayers on special occasions and national calls to prayer.

One of the most heartening signs is the broadening interest in prayer for healing; the number of prayer groups of various kinds, meeting regularly to pray for sick people, is impressive; alongside this, more and more churches are in specific ways concentrating on the sick and suffering, often on named persons. Increasingly, healing services focus on the healing of the person, making *the person* whole, sustaining, upholding, blessing, encouraging that alignment which is the acceptance of unrevealed divine will, surrendered, unquestioning; all this is the very opposite of regarding miraculous healing as the main purpose of the prayer. Instantaneous healing sometimes takes place; now and then there are "miraculous" healings beyond all explaining. But these are rare occurrences. The church's new interpretations of its responsibilities towards the sick enable it to collaborate realistically with the medical profession, team-work long overdue. The scope is vast; mental illness, in particular, needs the care of physician, psychiatrist and priest, working as a team.

Individual prayer, man withdrawn in an atmosphere which helps him to listen as well as to speak, this is an enriching of life, seldom, at the outset, recognized as that; persevering apprenticeship precedes the discovery that prayer is a powerhouse. The discovery changes one's attitude to prayer. It doesn't end the experience of prayer bringing no response; always we shall face arid periods, periods when prayer calls for every discipline, and times when it becomes impossible. But once the "power-house" experience, the invigorating, guiding, reassuring has become a proved experience, particularly in crisis and in prolonged ordeal, there is certainty beyond doubting that the potency is real. And the key to it, the first need, is the withdrawing—withdrawing at times into quiet, for strangely enough, what we are in need of can come sometimes in atmosphere, without our speaking, with no identifiable directions, no response, but the awareness sure, calming, and even serene.

Today's tensions, affecting nearly every aspect of our living, have broadened the interest in retreats, which provide opportunities for quiet, for silence, for prayer in conditions uninterrupted by normal daily routine. "The essence of retreat is to be with God in silence. The silence must be complete, . . . Go deep into the relaxation and peace of silence . . . this peace will not be emptiness, because God is here, and the imagination, the affections and the will are drawn towards God in the silence. The rest, while remaining truly a rest, will become quite effortlessly and unselfconsciously a rest *towards God*." This, from the present Archbishop of Canterbury, Dr. Ramsey.[4]

Silent prayer is probably the least known form of prayer to the vast majority of people, and the most effective to thousands who have persevered with its disciplines, which encourage a mental attitude—not as defined as thought—towards the God who is beyond all image, a reverent yearning, leading at times to "knowing God" through adoration, the intellect left behind. And because it is left behind, the intellect cannot hinder complete and fruitful experiences of this kind being shared by simple folk.

The reality and vividness of these experiences can help us to value inaction in times of stress and crisis, activity at these times being so frequently tense and exhausting. "Do not exhaust yourself by making efforts," writes Dom John Chapman, in a letter to a nun, "you seem still to think that you can make yourself good! You can't. But God can, and will, though slowly, perhaps. We can prevent His action—we can get in His way——"[5]

Those who submit to the disciplines of prayer have to face bleak periods, sterile days, times when prayer is ineffectual— and still persevere. "What I have learnt," wrote St. Teresa of Avila, "is that the entire edifice of prayer must be founded on humility . . . we should not worry ourselves to death even if we cannot think a single good thought."[6]

The bleakness, the arid periods inseparable from spiritual searching, should condition us for failures in prayer which we are inclined to interpret as something for which we are to blame. In many cases, we are, of course, emphatically to blame; if we know the disciplines to be essential, and shirk them, we rob ourselves of peace and deprive ourselves of the relationship which is prayer. But failure (i.e. what appears to us to be failure) is often God's will for us, one of the most difficult things to accept; through our seeming failures and sometimes in that way only, He can bring us farther along the road. All our striving seems nullified, until we remember that there are times when striving itself defeats the objects attainable only by surrender.

Which makes apparent failure less disturbing; and the saints go further—they prepare us for the mystery of the times when God seems to withdraw, to leave us to fail and falter and stumble. "God withdraws intermittently," writes Eckhardt, one of the best known mystics, "He hides himself from time to time—He is like a trustworthy physician. The withdrawal does not depend on you but upon Him whose act it is. He reveals Himself or not as He thinks best for you. It is up to Him to show himself or not as He thinks best for you, . . . according as He knows you are ready for him, for God is not a destroyer of nature but rather one who fulfils it, and He does this more and more as you are prepared."[7]

Maybe we need reminders of our depending; maybe only

God's withdrawal is adequate reminder of how we should nourish the spirit with prayer at its most exalting, purifying levels, prayer as Jeremy Taylor described it about three hundred years ago— "Prayer is the peace of our spirit, the stillness of our thoughts, the evenness of recollection, the seat of meditation, the rest of our cares and the calm of our tempest; prayer is the issue of a quiet mind, of untroubled thoughts, it is the daughter of charity and the sister of meekness."

Through Dorfs' ordeal, prayer of this kind became intensified; it became for her a relationship rather than exercise, discipline or duty, something which channelled spiritual nourishment to her. In its most perfect interpretation, prayer is that—a relationship. It is specifically tree and branch relationship—"I am the vine, ye are the branches." It ensures precisely that kind of nourishing—from the tree into the branch; that kind of discipline too, "Every fruiting branch he cleans, to make it more fruitful still." The tree and branch relationship implies utter dependence, for the nourishing and for the flourishing—"Without me, ye can do nothing."

Dorfs and I rarely discussed religion except when it cropped up in general conversation, but we each knew intimately and with no misgivings where the other stood and it was one of the many blessings of our long, happy married life that this was common ground. Because we both believed in prayer we mutually recognized its nourishment and upholding during the ordeal; I cannot remember that this was ever discussed between us, so perfect was our understanding. In the clarity of her outlook we found new evidence that we pray rightly when, in ordeal, we pray to be released *if that is possible within the divine purpose for us.* She never rebelled. The freedom of her heart, unswerving in its allegiance, was freedom from resentment and from the corrosion of bitternesss.

This freedom, fought for and won, was both infectious and creative. It lifted us all out of the doldrums, banished all our waverings, swept us into the harmony which is gladness, joy in living, praise. Praise is an infectious tonic which can rob a crisis of fear. It is a turning to the light; a salute, the response of the soul to its Creator and to the wonders of creation. This is the saints' interpretation of attack being the best form of defence—instant flight into praise, its dynamic changing fear and anxiety into faith and serenity. Filled with praise, the venturing mind can often gain a victory without directly encountering the enemy; the filling becomes a sweeping away of clouds of worry and foreboding. The very act of praise can be a triumph over fear; instead of searching for ways to defeat fear, we can replace it. It can be ousted by the replacing; for praise is a scattering and dissipating of blackness, gloom and defeat.

Here are gateways into power, illimitable and inexhaustible, and into the sublime relationship of a Father who is Love and children whose greatest need is love. And we are all children.

# IX

## TOLERATION

I see the different faiths of men as a circle, in the centre of which stands Truth. The nearer each one gets to Truth the closer they will be drawn to one another.

LORD SAMUEL

At an international Anglican Congress in Toronto in 1963, attended by 1,200 delegates from all over the world, the General Secretary of the Church Missionary Society insisted that God may reveal His truth through men of other faiths, or of no faith at all, and suggested Karl Marx and Sigmund Freud as specific examples of this.

Pointed enough; fair evidence that toleration is the spirit of the age. Loyalty to a religion no longer implies hostility to other religions, or to people with no religion, or even to people who challenge religion of any kind. When nations are jostling each other as intimately as Victorian street-neighbours, it is sheer bigotry to cling to the Victorian notion that all are heathens, all are damned, who are not of your own religion. The bitter hatreds between religions, inflamed by wars, show signs of withering, the spirit of toleration proving to be more effective than the spirit of hate. After centuries of hostility, the great religions are being presented to men's minds with changed emphasis, the new focus being on what is common ground, instead of all that separates them.

The background of this dramatic reversal, the upsurge and the resulting re-birth of toleration, is, of course, the volcanic history of our first half-century. The end of the Second World War found the nations exhausted and men disillusioned. The burden of shaping a new world fell mainly on those, mostly elderly, who had witnessed the slow and painful recovery after the First World War; then, they were young, the pioneering spirit was still sustained by ideals which had inspired and accounted for the unimaginable endurance of nations and men in concluding a seemingly endless struggle; universal longings for peace had seemed to justify the hope that peace could emerge.

But in 1945 there seemed no one to turn to. Disillusionment was so complete that many people lost heart. Lost heart to such a degree that they lost not only heart, but faith, faith in God as well as faith in governments. Circumstances made it all too easy to turn to the worship of the golden calf. On both sides of the Atlantic, machinery multiplied fantastically during the war was ready to produce "ploughshares instead of swords." Exploitation and ruthlessness fashioned the cradle of the affluent society in which was born the infant prodigy, modern man, self-centred and self-sufficient. After every war moral laxity is rife; after this war, morality seemed dethroned, ignored, abandoned. Twenty years later, unease in man's unsatisfied soul compels him to rouse himself to a new awareness of his situation. Not even the cacophony and the focus on acquisitiveness has blinded him to horizons or deafened him to the call of the pioneer in him; hardly conscious of the significance of what he is doing, he is prospecting for peace in revolutionary ways, toleration being a dominant keynote, toleration in religion, in communal, international, and racial relationships. Terror of the bomb is a spur. Only when they face common peril have nations effectively co-operated; prosperity's ugly child, jealousy, drives them into hideous separation.

Terror of annihilation by the bomb, added to disillusionment after two world wars, is propelling men towards neighbourliness; toleration is the implementing of it. Allegiance to one's native religion is seen no longer to make sense if it shuts out the possibility of there being other religions. Since the war this line of thought has received much encouragement. The Dean of St. Paul's writes:

"The most fruitful way of comparing religions with one another is to concentrate attention on their highest expressions and on their profoundest thoughts. When we do so, we discover that though they differ in important respects, they agree more than appears on the surface. A recent book, *On the Eightfold Way*, which is a study of Buddhism and Christianity, shows that the two religions are close to each other in many of their insights into the nature of human personality. And indeed it would not be widely far from the mark to say that all the great religions teach that men are living in illusion—and particularly in illusion about themselves."[1]

Shortly after the war, Aldous Huxley pin-pointed the striking resemblances of religious traditions shared by Christians, Buddhists, Hindus and Mohammedans, and summarized by saying:

"In regard to man's final end, all the higher religions are in complete agreement. The purpose of human life is the discovery of Truth, the unitive knowledge of the Godhead."[2]

Man's need to be instinctively aware of the existence of something beyond his capacity to understand does not therefore compel him to believe in the God of the Christian religion. Very gradually we are learning that exclusivity in religious belief, the shutting out of other beliefs, must give way to whatever unity will range men together against tyranny and persecution, range them for human dignity and its high potentialities.

The need for transcendence, man's inexpressible need for something outside himself, is universal; this is a unifying principle in the search for common ground among the great historic religions of the world. The common factors can never be adequately contained in documents, for controversy is endless; some of these factors relate to the kneeling, the adoration and the surrender, all making possible the forgiving, the replenishing and the sustaining, without which religion has no meaning. Theologians will wisely continue to search for common ground. The heartening progress in the overdue approaches to unity on the organizational side is probably more significant than we dare believe. We rightly use materialism as the label for most of what is the

D

enemy of religion. So successful is the invasion of materialism that we need the aggregated forces of the great religions, massed as a monolithic and dynamic weapon, to challenge and rebut it.

The spirit of man, subdued, terrorized, humiliated, vanquished for long, agonized periods is unquenchable and it is this spirit alone which can ultimately triumph over materialism—the universality of the spirit transcending all creed and dogma, the spirit of man recognizing the ineffectiveness of his boasted self-sufficiency. Religion is "of the spirit" and the spirit cannot be organized. Unity of the spirit, the ultimate unity, is immeasurably wider and deeper than all that could ever be achieved by organizational unity alone, but intensified effort to achieve organizational unity is needed, to quicken the urge towards unity of the spirit. In addition to the organizations, we need the seers and the prophets, pointing us to realms of thought beyond the confines of all societies. When our striving towards the new goal is reflected in our way of living, we shall merit the esteem of the emergent nations, not surprisingly dazzled today as they witness the religion of their former overlords subordinated to the economic prosperity race. Fortunately, there are, up and down the land, many crowded churches and dedicated parsons, defending the inviolable sanctity of the truth unshackled from denominationalism and presented with uncompromising courage, bringing men nearer to an understanding of the bond between sacrifice and love. "The manifestation of love," wrote William Temple, "by which it wins its response, is always sacrifice—when love is returned, th' sacrifice is the most joyful thing in the world, and heaven is ' e life of joyful sacrifice."[3]

Towards this conception of unity, love being its found ion, its guide and impetus, Pope John's contribution may co to be the most significant yet recorded in this century. Barri s fell as he cleared the ground for discussions—with the Anglic ι and the Orthodox churches, with other religions, and most notable of all, with Communism. The Pope made clear, time and time again, his wish that men should begin to study whatever is common

ground among them. Diversity is indispensable; mutual en-
lightenment emerges out of compared study in the spirit of
reconciliation; there are many aspects and manifestations of truth,
which alone is impregnable. In less than half a dozen years, Pope
John swept away centuries of feuds which had thwarted progress
towards the unity which can end so many deep, ancient quarrels,
winds of healing at last beginning to replace the gusts and
bluster of acrimony. When Buddhists found friendliness in the
Vatican some rusty shackles fell away. Sacrificial love is an
effectual ointment for old scars; out of chaos, we are heading for
cohesion. Slow though progress will often seem, with formidable
setbacks, and all the resisting of prejudice, direction has changed.
Time's kiss, after long frowning, may, who knows, be speeding
us towards exciting horizons; maybe the nameless pioneers are
already hacking their way through the dense undergrowth,
clearing paths to the hills.

Already compassion is ousting condemnation in the attitudes
of religion towards the self-styled irreligious. The swing from
"they who are not with us are against us" to "they who are not
against us are for us" is a new and positive focus, stressing the
possibility of sharing, loyalties to creed and dogma no longer
prohibiting the sharing. So many obstacles seem to be stupid,
then non-existent; everyone feeling cleaner when prejudices are
discarded, obsessional beliefs replaced by obsessional love, the
love which becomes compulsive in loving all who feel to be
"outside," even the self-abandoned and those abandoned or
scorned by society, the love giving them new hope. Caring for
people, the primary manifestation of love and the essence of
religion, cancels the need for so many arguments; arguments
about slum-clearance, the colour-bar, the chastity-charity problems, these and so many others are less formidable when exploitation and self-indulgence are realistically tested by the caring
which is not at all the emotional effervescence labelled as love in
tin-pan-alley, but love of a kind that tin-pan-alley has never
known. Only here and there can we hope to find major changes;

what is beyond challenging is that hunger for the compassion and the caring is finding new responses, establishing new common ground between believers and unbelievers, the committed and those who boast of not being committed, the evolutionists and the revolutionists, people of every religion and of none, ready to share new problems and new ways of coping with them, emerging out of common peril.

And notable among the new ways of tackling human problems is the "new science" as it has been called, of the psychiatrist and the psycho-analyst and the psychologist. Only its contemporary interpretations and its discoveries relating to this century's mental and nervous disturbances are new. As a science it is centuries old, many of its techniques also being centuries old. But in this century of man bedevilled by his own mind, his torture aggravated by the tensions inseparable from today's rhythms, once again, "the hour has produced the men." The immeasurable relief given to mental and nervous sufferers by the discoveries of Freud, Jung and their followers makes it unintelligent to spotlight only the sections of their writings which seem antagonistic to religion. Jung has over and over again testified to the paramount need for religion, evidenced in a lifetime's research and practice. The present chapter opened with recognition by an Anglican that Freud's teaching might constitute acceptable evidence in exploring new ways of conveying to man what religion can mean to him.

Psychiatry, psycho-analysis and psychology—grouping them, for convenience, as one branch of science—help many people to come to terms with life, to solve some problems, to find ways of living with many unsolved and possibly insoluble problems. True it is that they often seem to encourage self-expression at the expense of discipline. Much there is which may in some cases spotlight the ego; there seems at times to be little of renunciation. These are evidences of a science groping its way; in uncharted territory the diversity of experiment unavoidably includes much that will be scrapped as research is extended. Inevitably, a science relating to human behaviour will be in conflict with religion if it ignores religion or rejects it, but it is all too easy to forget that a scientist speaks most usefully when he speaks as a scientist.

The approach of this branch of science, trying to restore man to wholeness, differs in important ways from the approach of the churches, trying to restore man to his holiness, yet they are surely destined to operate in double harness, healing the mind and healing the spirit, which are not separate compartments in man's make-up, but a mass of intertwining strands. In an epoch of desperate loneliness, one of the heartening evidences of the new toleration is the reaching out of parson and "psycho", each more ready to discuss with the other the human problems which increasingly demand their collaboration.

Not less striking is the new evidence of toleration between religion and the agnostics and the humanists, all of whom believe in the potency of love, in love as the conditioning force in society, which is vacillating, unsure, apathetic, directionless where love is least evident. More interesting still, all these, religion, agnosticism, humanism are finding sufficient common ground to place more emphasis on what they share, and less on what divides them. Who could have imagined, until recently, that the President of the Humanist Society (Sir Julian Huxley) would feel justified in the magnanimity of writing this:

"Religion in some form is universal in human societies. Religions are man's organs for dealing with the problems of his destiny . . . many phenomena are charged with a magical quality of transcendent or even compulsive power over our minds, and introduce us to realms beyond ordinary experience. They merit a special designation: for want of a better, I use the term *divine*, though this quality of divinity is not supernatural but *transnatural*. The divine is what man finds worthy of adoration, that which compels his awe."

After outlining the concept of a humanist religion, he states that it will "enlist the aid of science in helping men and women to explore the depths and heights of their own inner selves instead of dissipating their energies in the restless pursuit of external novelty, and to realize more of their mental, physical and spiritual possibilities."[4]

Sir Julian has given further significant evidence of this spirit of toleration, by writing the introduction to a book written by a Roman Catholic priest, in which he says of the author, Pierre Teilhard de Chardin:

". . . he has forced theologians to view their ideas in the new perspective of evolution, and scientists to see the spiritual implications of their knowledge. He has both clarified and unified our vision of reality. In the light of that new comprehension, it is no longer possible to maintain that science and religion must operate in thought-tight compartments or concern separate sectors of life; they are both relevant to the whole of human existence. The religiously-minded can no longer turn their backs upon the natural world, or seek escape from its imperfections in a supernatural world; nor can the materialistically-minded deny importance to spiritual experience and religious feeling."[5]

Remote from the world's highway, a woman deprived of a long, calm evening of her life found much to hearten her, much to inspire, as she contemplated many encouraging evidences of toleration. We had come through two world wars, witnessed the idealistic urge of 1914 and the disillusionment after the second cataclysm. During the long vigil, the uneasy twenty years' armistice, the seemingly hopeless outlook for real peace, we had been spared bitterness, never ceasing to believe that eventually there would be born out of the long agony a world in which neighbourliness would again become real. In Dorfs' valuations, neighbourliness had always ranked high, the neighbourliness which is such a practical expression of toleration.

Ordinary men and statesmen, exploring common problems with neighbours, often find that fences are removed and barriers fall. After our perilous half-century it may be less difficult to discover common ground than when prosperity at the century's dawn, unthreatened by peril, was fanning the fires of jealousy and hate. Dare we hope that the threat of annihilation may, like world-wars and many other catastrophes, drive us into caring for each other?

# X

## THE CHANNEL

We did not feel as if our ordinary self was in communication with the Divine Spirit, but rather as if the Divine Spirit had for the time being transformed our personality, raising it to a higher state in which it could breathe a purer air than that of earth, and see something of the invisible.

DEAN INGE

LIKE THE TIDES, and the rhythm of the seasons, institutional religion's history is of its ebb and flow. At the ebb, forsaken man is impoverished, rudderless, hungry. Dark indeed are some of the chapters, the spirit of religion seeming to lose vitality or its power to evoke the human response which is its own enlivening; at times the church's temporal power has invaded its essentially spiritual sphere; or stewardship responsibilities have been misinterpreted by the clergy; or worse, involving laity as well as clergy.

Then, in the shadows, an apparently insignificant number of the forlorn discover all over again how individual an affair communion with the divine really is; at such times there may be no liturgy used, no formal service, no community; only isolated souls groping and finding in new ways that God can be as near, as potent, as loving, as responsive to an individual as to a congregation.

It almost seems that the ebb, so sparsely recorded, is one of the most enriching stages in the human pilgrimage; man in his alone-ness as well as his loneliness, uttering his cry and receiving the divine response. Maybe the heart of the matter can be most vitally experienced when the candle is flickering, never quite extinguished, yet hardly noticeable in the vast blackness. Candles, like stars, have a persisting brightness, consoling, reassuring, and guiding, penetrating the black however black it may be, and with unmistakable clarity pin-pointing the direction of hope. Across the centuries, a few candle-flames continue to illuminate. Men here and there are re-discovering the vitality of evidence bequeathed by the mystics. For that is what they are.

Mysticism is often confused with magic, with occultism, with spiritualism, with trances and ecstasy and psychic phenomena, and with messages from another world. It is not essentially like any of these. Union of the human spirit with the divine, that is what mysticism is about; it is concerned with the non-intellectual idea of love as the dominating, permeating influence which can enable man, through grace and humility, to live in the atmosphere and rhythm of divine love, subordinating his worldly interests. His ego is dethroned. His personality is changed as he surrenders more and more completely, for union is a process of receiving, not of achieving. Mysticism implies dedication, but contrary to popular belief, it is not a life narrowed by asceticism; what eventually transpires is the precise opposite—added zest and joy of the kind which includes merriment. Liberated, emancipated, the mystics cling uncompromisingly to a single purpose, which sustains them in persecution and can make martyrdom exultant. This, to which few attain, is man at his noblest, identified with his God. Mysticism does not necessarily imply either the mind of a saint or the mind of a poet. Lacking the mental discipline of a saint, or the schooling of a poet's mind, we ordinary folk can, through discipline and silence, lay ourselves open to this pervading influence: ". . . the more ordinary souls who say they do know God's existence directly, neither by faith nor argument, are perhaps fairly common; and there is no reason why they should be disbelieved; for the same seems to be true of many who practise contemplative prayer, just as it is true of some of the great mystics —that their experience is definite though incommunicable."—so writes Dom John Chapman, in his famous book of letters.[1]

Some of the profound mystics have lived and died as obscure, ordinary men made "extraordinary" by the quality of their dedicated living. "Though they were only a minority, there was no lack of devout laymen in the fourteenth century. It was the age of the mystic recluse, both clerical and lay, but particularly the latter—who, withdrawing from the world to a life of religious contemplation, found in the inner experience of the heart a new revelation."[2]

In the fourteenth and fifteenth centuries mysticism was nourished by revulsion from a world of turmoil, strife, war and wickedness. It was to be one of the most fruitful, most creative periods in the history of mysticism. Revulsion against the world meant retirement from it; there was no alternative. We are passing through a somewhat comparable phase, characterized by excesses—war, cold and hot, sexual licence, self-indulgence, acquisitiveness, ruthlessness. Whereas in medieval times there was no satisfactory alternative to complete withdrawal from the world, this century needs—in addition to mystics—people who, instead of withdrawing from the world, live in it without becoming too involved. Convinced of the incomparable satisfactions of the mystical life, they would yet never claim to be mystics; sometimes they become channels through which spiritual energy can be transmitted. They are of all creeds and of none. They believe in the dignity of man, in that highest in him which not even the massive commercial exploitation of his most earthy frailties can annihilate, and they know, with no uncertainties, that without loyalty to spiritual values, life is thwarted and warped.

Humility being their anchorage, these people strive to live what they believe, failure on failure being part of their discipline. Now and then they can provide an oasis, share serenity, point to horizons. A broken-hearted world which has lost its way, starved of compassion, too often near despair, has perhaps, by its very need, bred them for its own rescue. As a contemporary pioneer puts it, "Why should there not be men vowed to the task of exemplifying, by their lives, the general sanctification of human endeavour?—men whose common religious ideal would be to give a full and conscious explanation of the divine possibilities or demands which any worldly occupation implies—men, in a word, who would devote themselves, in the fields of thought, art, industry, commerce and politics, etc., to carrying out in the sublime spirit these demands—the basic tasks which form the very bonework of human society?"[3]

From the mystics, such people learn much of their patterning. The mystics, unshaken by tragedy, are acquainted with silence of a kind which creates the possibility of union with the divine. They are nourished and upheld by inner peace, in part the outcome of silence. The rhythm of their living is tuned to the divine. We can learn from them, aware of being able only to glimpse the horizons.

A friend recounted to me an experience in a Belgian church which had lasting effects on him. A nun entered, knelt, and extended her arms, cruciform, remaining perfectly still for a long time. The impression on my friend's mind was incised so deeply that it recurred, time and again. It was his first experience of this kind; about a year later, he was suddenly impelled, before dawn one morning, to lie on his back in bed, extend his arms and as he put it "try to eliminate himself and become utterly blank and receptive." He began to make this a daily exercise, eventually finding that a simple verse had spontaneously formed in his mind; he described it as his "focussing point":

> "Imprint Your love, Your suffering if You will,
>   And teach me, O my Lord, how to be still.
>   Imprint Your joy, and take away my fear,
>   And in the silence, let me feel You near."

In later conversations, he told me that he never repeated these lines except when lying flat on his back, lying cruciform, relaxed, looking upward (but with his eyes closed), trying to look into infinity and freeing himself from distracting thoughts by concentrating on this verse.

All this led to a number of talks; encouraged, I questioned him more and more closely. A door seemed to open through which I could occasionally catch a glimpse of something intensely significant. Here are the notes I made during these conversations:

1. Until he became conscious not only of relaxation but of

surrender which he described as "nothingness" he waited in silence, then, very slowly he began—"Imprint Your love."

2. Sometimes he did this in mornings, just before rising, sometimes last thing before going to sleep. And if he repeated it when he happened to be awake during the night, the experience was intensified by an awareness that the world was at any rate relatively silent and asleep.

3. Often this led directly into silence, varying in duration except for morning, when the day's programme had a timing. Evening became his chosen time when possible; the very idea of separating himself from the timing of clocks seeming to facilitate his penetration into a different realm.

4. The words were repeated at varying speeds, but always slowly; sometimes with lengthy pauses, almost unintentional. There might be only a word or two, then prolonged silence.

5. Usually he found himself lingering over the phrase "be still." His awareness of the capacity for real stillness had increased with the recognition that "distractions are destruction" as he put it. When I questioned him further on this it became clear that he regarded his "apprenticeship" as arduous, the perseverance required being far more disciplined than he had ever imagined; and he had never realized that he could not "be still" in the sense used here until his daily exercise disillusioned him.

6. There had been what he called a "negative gain." After much disappointment he had come to recognize aridity and lack of response in himself. A sense of frustration was inevitable and even more than that: it became accepted as the "black night" which the mystics tell us is a common experience. Conversely, there were many occasions when, he said, "dynamic" was his only word to describe the silence; he was convinced that this kind of silence was creative in his own daily living. The idea of results is alien to this silence, which is subjective. You are not asking for anything beyond what is implied in surrender. Serenity, a "fruition" sometimes of silence, cannot be expected, but one might find that like dew, it descends. It is the kind of

serenity which is granted to some through suffering borne with fortitude, through selfless living, through that indefinable harmony with the divine which is so rare.

7. Referring on one occasion to creative, dynamic silence, he said he had found preparatory periods most rewarding. Lying on his back, gradually achieving relaxation of both mind and body, he had found a contentment in the very relaxing; "sinking into something"—that was how he described what is so difficult to describe, and he had wondered sometimes if that contentment, without the specific effort to achieve silence, was a preliminary to what the mystics refer to as bliss. He conceived bliss as union with the divine. He regarded it as something for which probably he could not hope, yet at the same time, something which might one day become an experience, as unexpected as the dynamic silence.

8. It had surprised him, he said, to find how few people appeared to know anything about a subject which to him had become increasingly significant. This prompted me to make enquiries among the very few friends who might conceivably have some contribution to make on the general subject.

"You will find," said one friend, "that your guess is right; few people are seriously interested in what is called "the Silence." Browning may have sounded arrogant when he wrote that "God has a few of us whom He whispers in the ear," but it is only too true and the reason is devastatingly simple—unless you are prepared to listen, you can't hear the whisper. "And the whisper," continued my friend, "is not a whisper of the kind we know, and certainly it is nothing occult; it is perhaps a vibration; or maybe you are listening to silence. This can govern your thinking, condition your living and add up to a simple working philosophy, essentially different from the philosophies of the learned, yet far more useful to ordinary folk, who are more interested in living than in reading about how to live."

Another friend suggested that H. T. Hamblin's book, *My*

*Search for Truth*, might include something important on this subject. The book is autobiographical. Hamblin was a successful business-man who threw everything over in order to live a dedicated life, spent largely in writing. When he died in 1958, one of his associates wrote:

"At a time when men and women were failing to find in orthodox religion the Bread and the living Water he was a pioneer who cleared the choked springs for them. Always very clear in his vision, he was alert always to the spurious, the "fancy" cults, the glamorous and sensational by-paths which lead the beginner astray, and his common sense was outstanding. His eyes were on the stars, for he was of the line of mystics of all ages and creeds, but his feet remained firm in the world."[4]

"For many years," wrote Hamblin, "I tried to enter the Silence —but in vain. I often read about it, but could not find it—for one thing, no two writers seemed to agree as to what the Silence was. Some seemed to think that it was a kind of trance; others taught that it was simply inhibiting all thought, thus making the mind a blank; yet others again said that it was a state of negative passivity or a sinking down into a state of dreamy self-hypnotism. None of these methods would bear examination. . . . All at once I realized that it was my trying so hard that was hindering me, and that if I would cease my efforts, then I should find that already I was in the Silence. . . . What we have to do is to stop our fruitless strivings, and instead rest in the love of God. . . ."[5]

In a later chapter he takes us into the depths of his personal experience:

"Our loftiest thoughts about God are only hindrances now; they have served us well hitherto, but now they have to be cast aside because any thought about God is limiting, not only to us but also to God. In one sense, of course, it is impossible to limit

God in any way for He is limitless, but we can limit Him, as far as we are concerned, by our thought. God is infinitely beyond thought, therefore our thoughts about God limit Him to our thought. . . . The God who can be named is not the Ineffable One, but as it were a God of our own limitations.

"As we move forward towards the Ineffable, we lay aside all names and forms; we also emerge beyond all thoughts and ideas about God. Consequently, because we cease trying to limit the Limitless, it begins to become possible for us to go forward. All forms, thoughts, names and ideas have to be laid aside by us. So as they arise, we gently brush them aside and continue steadily forward to That which transcends all forms, thoughts, names and ideas. And so we move forward to the Nameless, Ineffable One. We discard everything until at last we come to Nothing. . . . And when we have come to Nothing—we find that we have found Everything."[6]

This kind of silence, tranquil, relaxed, can enable us, after the school of self-discipline coupled with determination, to discover that our own thinking can unmistakably come under the influence of indefinable harmony. Emerging from that influence there can come new clarity of thought, *provided we do not seek solutions to specific problems*. The experience can bring a sense of direction, a feeling of security, confidence overcoming fear.

But how, in the mounting tensions of every-day life and the invading distractions, can we make time for silence, *any* kind of silence, involving stern discipline, or even for the deep quiet which is its antechamber? One answer is that we make time for what we want to do—what we are resolved to do. So we have to decide if it is worth while, the discipline, the surrender, the arduous apprenticeship. The deep quiet which leads into energizing silence can yield no harvest without surrender as the primary discipline. After long apprenticeship we may be able to retire into fruitful silence at odd moments, shedding anxiety and strain. Years may pass before we feel to be using it adequately;

it can be a scouring, ridding us of the clinging passions of a clamorous world, and a cleansing, ridding us of self-indulgence, bringing us back to sane valuations; a refuge when fury sends us flying, when din becomes intolerable, when the utmost gentleness of a human voice is so much less gentle than silence.

This is the gold of silence, treasure which increases as we use it, treasure demanding no intelligence test, for by nature it is unworldly, projecting us into a different world, momentarily, or for time long or short, seeming never too long. Even in the early stages, practice intensifies the replenishing which withdrawal from activity, from noise and from all that is part of the day's programme can bring.

Learning now that this silence is not a gap between activities, we can discover that it is its own activity; then, finding, to our astonishment, that in silence we can not only listen, but hear, the activity becomes creative. We begin to listen and to hear with hitherto unimagined zest; what we hear seems often different, due to its setting, surrounded now by silence *and even becoming a part of silence*. We find ourselves welcoming opportunities for silence, cherishing them so much that ruthlessly we carve them out of the full days; the quality of the day's living becomes enhanced, and most of all when the enhancing is the healing peculiar to silence.

This, we came to know, to prize; more and more, as time passed, we came to depend on its nourishing. For Dorfs had become a channel.

# XI

## THE LAST MONTHS

> O painful labour.
> Labour beyond all strength. And you performed it
> day after day, you dragged yourself along to it
> and pulled the lovely woof out of the loom
> and wove your threads into another pattern.
> And still had spirit for a festival.
>
> RAINER MARIA RILKE

sufferings is, in infinitely gentle, tender ways, longing to help those less fortunate. But it is hardly possible to exaggerate the benefits of the shift of focus, away from one's self. Undoubtedly, this accounts for the relative freedom from illness of many people, in particular the poor, who "have no time to be ill." It is in part the explanation of the surprisingly high general health standards during world wars; bombing and rescue, shared hardships and community problems left little room for brooding.

All this was confirmed by Dorfs' complete refusal to concentrate on her illness; it could not cloud a life suffused by light. And this emancipation from one's self, from one's troubles which could so easily have captured the days, is less an attempt to free one's self than to leave one's self out, by concentrating on other things, other people, which makes it easier to understand that the sick, and especially those gravely ill, can so often lighten the load of other sufferers. Man does not live by bread alone; in so many ways he can be sustained, nourished, brought to the serenity which no longer demands release from suffering as a condition of allegiance, but can rise, exultant, even in pain. This nourishing is daily bread; we came to know with certainty that it would be provided, that it would include a diversity of things, the main parts of the loaf being courage and faith.

For long periods every day, prior to the last phase, Dorfs was alone. She not only loved those times, but needed them. In our forty years of married life we probably spent far more time together than the average; nearly always, we went on holiday together and to theatres, concerts and on other outings. Yet, with no need for explanation, but in perfect harmony and understanding, solitude was always accessible to either of us. We both needed it. That made mutual awareness of the need automatic. Often there seems to be imperfect understanding of this need in another for the solitude which tolerates no clock. We are individuals. For those who need solitude, starvation and a warping of life are the penalties of denying it; nourished by it, they can give more, in kindliness, gentleness and harmony.

When rights give place to needs, the give-and-take which is the essence of a good marriage is implemented by glad giving and grateful taking. Mutual recognition of solitude as a need can deepen companionship; quiet can at times become more eloquent than words. This is one of love's most precious manifestations; in this, as in other ways, our riches increased as the encroachment of disease became more obvious. Incommunicable assurance, coming to us through shared quiet and sometimes long silence, deepened our conviction that whilst the long shadows were growing darker, all was well. Timelessly, with no drag, these luminous days and hours slipped gently, almost imperceptibly away, assuring us of affinities refined and perfected through suffering, confirming in us something never committed to the clumsiness of words—the conviction that the partnership would continue into eternity. Its sureness was at no time invaded by doubt; the idea of physical separation, known to be inevitable, could be full of mystery, and it was, but no longer by doubts.

As the progress of the disease limited Dorfs' physical energy, these rich periods of shared quiet became longer, more frequent, more meaningful. Gratefully, we accepted what sometimes seemed like an unexpected benison. Laughingly we resented the breaking of the harmonious rhythm—for meals and medicines, for everything related to the mechanics of living, which had degenerated into trivialities.

Never was the shared quiet long enough. Never were we, either of us, assailed by restlessness. Tranquility had achieved new meaning. Increasingly we longed to escape into it, as to some island, isolated from the mainland, sheltered from storm.

For a long time the day had been our unit of time and, gradually, this had a calming effect. When you never know what the morrow may bring, save more intractable problems, each day becomes precious. Not only its ephemeral character and its fugitive opportunities realistically apprehended, but keenness to arrive at its ending in some worth while way, unashamed, and this seemed to enhance the quality of living as one day passed into the next. Each day a bonus; each day re-valuations. When each day is more uncertain than its predecessor, you can come to realize a largeness of opportunity. These days can bring a flowering of faith, which scorns complaining and somehow surrounds the day with an aura and with the splendour of shining jewels. On these days there can be high and memorable moments. And on cloudy days you find that it has become less difficult to discern silver linings. Resentment, you have long discarded, bitterness too; long ago you have come to distinguish, no longer uncertain, between the tinsel of life and its hard-won gold.

Is it, perhaps, this—that you have arrived at last at the point where you know that life and death are not, as maybe you once imagined them to be, a terminating, but a glorious continuity; chapters, not complete books?

For us, at any rate, all doubts had fled. And, as sometimes happens, love and sorrow had met on a road leading towards holiness.

# XII

## SALUTE

Calvary (we witnessed this),
Became for her
A daily celebration of her Lord,
Suffering; serene;
History's most costly triumph
Patterned in her humility.

AND SO, HER battles won, she came all serenely to her crowning.

Neither tragedy nor sorrow was in our minds. Radiantly she had acquitted herself of all that crucible or cross could demand. There had been no faltering. Up to the time when medical care gently dulled consciousness, her gaiety of spirit had pervaded her home. Nourished and upheld by channelled grace, of which she had been as fully aware as of the deep love in which she was enfolded, she had triumphed over fear. "I know," said her specialist, three days before she died, "but no visitor could possibly know, how very weak she is; this is a triumph of the human spirit."

How infinitely gentle Nature can be! Gentle beyond imagining. As the little boat crossed the bar, all our last anxieties were dispelled: utter tranquillity.

It seemed fitting to include in the newspaper announcements of her death, some signal to her friends that mourning would be a denial of all she had striven to achieve. In verses which have somehow survived the centuries, one couplet came to mind—verses written about 1,500 years ago, by Paulinus, a Roman governor and a poet. After Rome fell, he spent all he had in ransoming prisoners. The story is told by Helen Waddell in *The Wandering Scholars*.[1] "At the last moment came a poor widow, pleading for her only son. Paulinus' hands were empty, but he sold himself as a slave, bought back the boy, and was shipped with the rest of the slaves to Africa." Distilled into two lines of one of Paulinus' poems, this was all we needed to say:

"Triumphs the soul above its house in ruin,
        Deathless, begot of immortality."

In the little chapel where we gathered to salute her, all was praise: "Jesu, joy of man's desiring," then, in the brief service, prayers of special significance, followed by the final verses of the eighth chapter of Romans, chosen because they emphasize the idea of no separation. For many years, the concluding verse had been for us almost a creed:

"For I am persuaded that neither death nor life, nor angels, nor principalities, nor powers, nor things present, nor things to come, nor height, nor depth, nor any other creature, shall be able to separate us from the love of God, which is in Jesus Christ our Lord."

As we filed out, there was the organ-burst of "Praise to the holiest in the height," to Elgar's *Gerontius* setting; soaring through shafted sunlight, the echo was triumph indeed.

\*　　　　\*　　　　\*

Was Dorfs, then, a remarkably brave woman, inspirational in her acceptance of a terrifying assignment? The answer, of course, is "Yes." But that is only the beginning of the answer.

In the nobility of her character there had always been a sternness of self-discipline which contributed significantly to its nobility. Always, she had elected to stride courageously in conflict, deciding with no hesitancy, once she was sure of direction; when she faced major problems, there was no assessing of the sacrifice involved. Praise for herself she had always rejected, aware of its devitalization. "I cannot do my job," she said, "if people tell me I'm wonderful—they are feeling sorry for me—I'm not wonderful and I need every bit of discipline, and you must try to protect me from comments of that kind, because we shall all burst into tears, and we can't afford that, it's too exhausting; it is all so very kindly meant, and I do appreciate it, but we must avoid it."

The process of her decision when the ordeal confronted her is beyond knowing. It involved the sweat of Gethsemane, but there emerged the sublime calmness of the Gethsemane decision, irrevocable, terrifying, but utterly tranquil. Long after that, in the last days, when she so quietly said, "this is Calvary," the quietness was still a calmness; no plea, no desire to be spared, only an inarticulate, overwhelmingly expressive yearning to be upheld in what was beyond human resources to compass and to conquer. So easily there might then have descended on us all not only despair, but a feeling of the futility of the battling, of the hand of destiny against us, a withering of something vital to a courageous facing of the days. But from the early days in hospital she had schooled herself—"looking outwards and upwards"— "thinking positively and travelling hopefully."

Dorfs' experience contributed nothing to the study of miracles. There was no miracle. She made a slight but significant contribution to the study of acceptance and its consequences. The two opposing attitudes towards ordeal produce diametrically opposite states of mind, apart from the repercussions on other people. Out of acceptance come harmony and serenity; resentment lands us in anxiety, unease and discord. "We ought to go down on our knees," Dorfs said, after a year of suffering, "and thank God there is no resentment here."

For those who could not find their way, she was all compassion; for the embittered, the unforgiving, and most of all for those who are haunted by the ego. For this is man needing the infinite tenderness of compassion. We are difficult to rescue from the poignant struggle with our worst selves, the ego flaunting itself, arrogance masking the real person, delaying what has been called "the victory achieved . . . over all the pride which arises from self-assertion."[2] Behind the façade we despise ourselves for pretending self-sufficiency, for stifling the deep yearning for love. Self-deprecation is self-indulgence; when we become nauseated by its futility we can find direction towards self-esteem—self which is cleansed from disguised forms of self-pity.

"When the fight begins within himself,
A man's worth something. God stoops o'er his head,
Satan looks up between his feet—both tug—
He's left, himself, in the middle: the soul wakes
And grows.[3]

Deep compassion she felt, too, for all who suffer from obsessions. Sacrificial love, invading, can become an "unselfed"
obsession which drives out all other obsessions; there will no
longer be room for them. Focus is reversed; replacing that preoccupation with ourselves which is fear twin-linked with the
ego, this kind of love is not an escape from something, but, to
borrow a phrase from Keats, it is "breaking through the clouds,"
entry into a new world.

To misinterpret Dorfs' real contribution would be a dis-service
and it would deter some who might be inspired or sustained by
her example, so easily could they regard her case as a phenomenon.
The simple truth is that she was a very human, normal person,
doing a tragically heart-breaking job with heart and mind committed, even when the heart was breaking and the mind faced
impenetrable blackness. An ordinary person she was, who became
extraordinary when the encounter with fear, catastrophe and crisis
changed her by some irradiation of light, transmuting tragedy;
in that new perspective there is a new relationship to the reality
which we can dimly apprehend but cannot define. Here we are
at the heart of the matter. The remarkable thing was not the
person; it was the person's elected way of responding to a
challenge of which the significance was never in doubt. The
response was wholehearted, immediate, with no reservations.
From that moment she was a dedicated person. What she recognized as her assignment she would carry out with all the resources
at her command, all the courage she could muster and all that she
might, through discipline and in humility be enabled to receive;
for she never imagined her own resources to be more than a
fraction of the total resources available to her,—given true

acceptance. This was to be the crescendo, the culmination but not the end, not the tragedy but the triumph. No thought of self, which could only rob her of what, through self, was unattainable. Her temperament and her dedication seemed to demand something beyond victory itself: triumph, with its implication of majesty, range and sweep, glorious, shattering in its consequences. Even victory might be a near thing. This was to be beyond all uncertainty. Distress and pain and the fantastic deprivations, none of them affected her inflexible resolve. Not that the resolute acceptance and commitment freed her from physical suffering. Not at all. From such encounters, seemingly unremitting in their distress, this pilgrim was enabled to distil something. No alchemist ever changed more astonishingly a leaden thing into a golden thing, a dull thing into brightness; and the brightness here, beyond the achieving of alchemy, was radiance, so that the place of the pilgrimage was illumined, and the people who came to the place became aware of the radiance reaching across to them. Of such experiences they spoke by compulsion, amazed at the radiance, amazed that it came out of deep suffering and a sentence of death.

Gradually, the enveloping light, for such it seemed, became not less potent, but less mysterious; the unyielding discipline, the transmitting and the transmuting, were all the outcome of aligning the will with the divine will. Acceptance meant nothing less than this unconditional, freely-willed and unresenting exchange of the human will for the divine will. Was the cost envisaged? No one can know. But the decision made, was never revised. No challenging of what had so painfully to be endured as the cost of accepting. Deviating not a hairsbreadth, neither on the rare good days nor the days when there was little beyond enduring.

Clearer and clearer it became, as the pilgrimage was prolonged, that there was something indefinable constantly nourishing the human spirit. An imperturbable core of tranquillity made all questioning meaningless. Something was resistant even to pain.

It was as if the pain had become incidental, as indeed it had; its sting there, intense and intensified, but no longer its significance. For here was indestructible armour. History records it in every age, but all too rarely. This aligning of the will means that nothing matters save instant and unquerying acceptance of whatever seems, from day to day, to be the divine will. All else is subordinated to this. Desire, relief, peace itself, every manifestation of human longing, human choosing, human delight or joy or satisfaction, all these cease to tempt or to attract: it is as if they have ceased to exist. Life has been changed. Purpose is centred in the divine will. "The will of God," writes an eighteenth-century priest, "presents itself at each instant like an immense ocean which the desire of your heart cannot empty, although it will receive of that ocean the measure to which it can expand itself by faith, confidence and love. The whole of the created universe cannot fill your heart, which has a greater capacity than everything else that is not God. The mountains which affright your eyes are tiny as atoms to the heart. The divine will is an abyss, the opening of which is the present moment. Plunge into this abyss and you will find it ever deeper than your desires. Pay court to no one, do not worship illusions, they can neither enrich you nor deprive you of anything. The sole will of God will wholly fill you and leave you with no void; adore that will, go straight towards it, pierce through and abandon all external appearances. The stripping, death and destruction of the senses establish the reign of faith: the senses adore creatures, faith adores the divine will. Take away their idols from the senses, they weep like children in despair; but faith triumphs, for faith cannot be deprived of the will of God. When the event of the present moment terrifies, starves, strips and attacks all the senses, it is just at that moment that it nourishes, enriches and vitalizes faith, which laughs at the losses of the senses as the governor of an impregnable town laughs at useless attacks."[4]

This opens the flood-gates, to joy which is exultant, to the love which unceasingly demands to give, demands this more than it demands love itself. Scorning obstacles, it demands to give sacrificially, counting suffering as part of the sacrifice, part of the giving. Indeed, suffering and sacrifice are at the heart of it; giving with no counting of the cost, it gives all, and less than all it will not give.

Love continues to triumph even when triumph looks like defeat. This is logic's despair and the despair of all who are deluded by the masquerading of the villain, self-love, believing that he can ever become the hero, self-sufficiency.

Love such as this is a fire, gathering into itself all who would damp it, smother or stifle it. This love dares all; even in the agony of its suffering, it dares to envision horizons. No longer earth-bound, it soars, charting new ways out of human anguish.

# XIII

## ALIGNMENT

Where ask is have, where seek is find,
Where knock is open wide.
                    CHRISTOPHER SMART

S O THE HEART'S peace implies surrender; peace of soul as
well as peace of mind. There is a knocking at the door, which
we are never compelled to open. There is a task, an assignment; we need not accept it. But acceptance, the answering of
the knock on the door, must be more than surrender; the surrender must be unconditional. Alignment with the divine will,
nothing less.

Out of blackness and fog and fear, this road leads to serenity.
Daily, maybe, fear has to be encountered and overcome. Challenge accepted means the refining in the crucible and the
hammering of the gold. Triumph is made possible because we
are *brought through*, our puny resources, all we thought we could
count on, being replaced by inexhaustible resources, adequate
for no-matter-what, unquestioned and beyond all doubting.
Test by ordeal is as adequate as it is unique; in this way, as in no
other way, frail humanity can apprehend the seeming miracle.

Even failure can then be assessed as what it really is—a stepping-
stone. Why do failures so easily rob us of faith? Does worth-while
success ever come with trial and error, without many failures,
without failures which at the time, appear final, conclusive, an
end to hope? Do we misinterpret the apparent failure which
culminated in Calvary, in chaos and in the death of hope? Isn't
the record plain—apparent triumph of despair being in reality
triumph *over* despair?

LORD, *I have been forgetting—*
*I have been forgetting how often You were frustrated; had I*
*remembered that, I would have offered my frustrations as a gift to*

*You. I remember, thinking about this quietly, what strange offerings You accept. It is all so difficult to understand, but now, remembering, I want to offer You things I could never offer, save for Your command.*

*I am kneeling, Lord; mentally, I am on my knees, for I must bow low when I offer You my failures and frustrations. I had forgotten, Lord, Your failures, all culminating, in the desertion in Gethsemane, in the hopelessness, the black despair of Calvary, the agony of Your cry, when being forsaken was all Your consciousness.*

*Forgive me, Lord, that I have been forgetting.*

*Forgive me for presuming that always I must overcome, always win all the battles, count as failures whatever I thought was not a success. Forgive me for not sharing Your forsaken-ness, Your last despair, the blackness and the bleakness of the day You knew to be Your last day.*

*Lord, I have been forgetting that Your command is not always to conquer, but sometimes to lose battles. So reluctantly I accept patient plodding. The loneliness of pilgrimage can become so disillusioning that I fail to recognize horizons—*

*—and to hear Your voice,*

*—and to cherish Your silence,*

*—and to choose rest, to be*
*   inactive, just to be.*

*Lord, I have been forgetting that loving You includes faltering, and listening without hearing, praying without any response, failing and failing and failing, and above all, failing to offer You something You have asked of me—my failures.*

*I am kneeling, Lord; my soul is on its knees, begging to be unforgetting, yearning to share Your hopelessness, Your nothingness which I shall never understand but which I no longer seek to understand.*

*I will remember, Lord, that sometimes my striving is a rebellion against You. I will remember how You could have defended Yourself, how you could have won; I will remember that the mystery of Your choosing to lose must remain impenetrable.*

*I will remember, Lord, that failure can sometimes be my only road to humility; that success would so often separate me from Your lowliness.*

*In the tenderness of Your compassion, Lord, help me on the grey days to remember that they are Your days; even when they remain grey, let me offer them as Your days.*

Alignment is a "coming through" to the functioning of the best in us; it involves freeing ourselves from what is secondary, however worthy that may be. Consciously, there has to be a jettisoning, a renouncing. Only in that way is the flourishing of the highest made possible, the maturing in that unmistakable rhythm in which we know, no longer unsure, that the person in us, enemy of the ego in us, can be fulfilled. Alignment consists of consciously choosing the inevitable, of which we have become aware with certainty beyond arguing; the choosing which sent Schweitzer, needed by civilized Europe, into the uncivilized African swamps, where he was even more needed; it is the choosing which commits men in every age to their destined and difficult assignments, the choosing which sent Jesus to Calvary. Deep down, we know when these fateful moments of decision come, or unsure, we can through disciplines and humility, become sure with utter clarity. How tempting to argue with ourselves, to discuss with others what we know to be beyond discussing, to busy ourselves, action becoming the smoke screen which can be dispelled only by the inaction which is deliberate withdrawal into stillness. Stillness prolonged into silence. Silence which enables us to hear.

Through agony the encounter may come. If it comes that way, the mystery of suffering may be illumined by serenity born out of the alignment. Yet neither agony nor suffering is an invariable element in alignment. What is essential is the kind of decision which can culminate in dedication.

This *kind* of impact on her world was Dorfs' significant contribution to it: interpreting and transmuting ordeal, with no lessening of its disciplines. Only in a limited sense could we know the dimension in which she was living; we knew she was enabled to accept adequate spiritual nourishment, that she was upheld by accepting it, that her surrender into the divine was the opposite of resignation into fate, becoming the effective evidence of her alignment with the divine purpose she was apparently destined to fulfil; that she came to regard herself only as a humble transmitter, used by the divine to encourage people who in various ways came in contact with her. This we felt compelled to interpret as the spirit affecting matter, the divine directing material affairs, transcending of a human problem through the dedication which is alignment.

Alignment means self-oblivion, a term used by Dag Hammarskjold, General Secretary of the United Nations, whose tragic death in Africa brought to light the simple elements of his philosophy and faith. Remembering the fantastic demands on his time, it is of particular interest to find that his reading included much written by the medieval mystics. "Love," he said, "meant for them simply an overflowing of strength with which they felt themselves filled when living in self-oblivion. And this love found natural expression in an unhesitant fulfilment of duty and in an unreserved acceptance of life, whatever it might bring them personally, of toil, suffering or happiness." He had himself discovered the way to harmony; he writes, "the explanation of how man should live a life of active social service in full harmony with himself as a member of the community of the spirit, I found in the writings of those great medieval mystics for whom 'self-surrender' had been the way to self-realization, and who in 'singleness of mind' and 'inwardness' had found strength to say yes to every demand which the needs of their neighbours made them face, and to say yes also to every fate life had in store for them when they followed the call of duty as they understood it."[1]

Hammarskjold's insistence on self-oblivion was shared by Archbishop Temple: "Humility," he wrote, "means that you feel yourself, as a different person, out of count, and give your whole mind and thought to the object to which they are directed.

. . . The humility which consists in being a great deal occupied about yourself and saying you are of little worth, is not Christian humility. It is one form of self-occupation, and a very poor and futile one at that; but real humility makes for effectiveness because it delivers a man from anxiety, and we all know that in all under-takings, from the smallest to the greatest, the chief source of feebleness is anxiety."[2]

The only book Hammarskjold had with him on that last fateful journey was Thomas à Kempis' *Imitation of Christ* which by the frequency of its new translations and re-printings continues, after centuries of study, to be widely accepted as a guide in contemporary thinking—and no wonder; its basic sanity is too real to be dated:

"Leave empty matters to the empty-headed. . . . Had you never gone out and listened to idle talk, you would the better have remained perfectly at peace."

"There is no man richer, more powerful or more free than he who can forsake himself."

"Man is not by nature inclined to carry the cross, to love the cross, to chasten the body, and bring it into subjection; to refuse honours, to submit to insults with goodwill, to despise himself, and welcome disparagement . . . if you trust in your own strength, you will be unable to achieve any of these things."

"None can live in love without suffering."

"Progress in the spiritual life consists not so much in enjoying the grace of consolation as in bearing its withdrawal with humility."

"Do not think that you have found true peace when you happen to experience no trouble."

"Self-love does you more harm than anything else in the world."

"Possess nothing that may hinder your spiritual progress, or rob you of inward freedom."

"If you want this thing or that, or to be here or there in order to satisfy your convenience and pleasure, you will never be at rest, nor free from care."

"At one time you are cheerful, at another sad; now peaceful, now troubled; now full of devotion, now wholly lacking it; now zealous, now slothful; now grave, now gay. But the wise man, who is well versed in spiritual matters, stands above these changing emotions."

"It is better to turn away from controversial matters, and leave everyone to hold their own opinions, than to belabour them with quarrelsome arguments."

"Whenever a man desires anything inordinately, at once he becomes restless. . . . Yet, if he obtains what he desires, his conscience is at once stricken by remorse, because he has yielded to his passion."

"If we rely only on the outward observances of religion, our devotion will rapidly wane."[3]

Hammarskjold's pilgrimage to harmony through self-oblivion was probably less arduous, and not as tempestuous, as was Beethoven's; both men arrived at self-oblivion, but they climbed different slopes of the mountain. In these extracts from his biography of Beethoven, J. W. N. Sullivan outlines Beethoven's journey towards alignment dramatically:

"Beethoven at this time greatly desired fame. His genius was to be exploited for his personal glory. He had not yet reached the position of seeing himself rather as a priest than as a king. His general attitude is exhibited in one of his arrogantly humorous letters to Court Secretary Von Smeskall. 'The devil take you,' he says. 'I don't want to know anything about your whole system of ethics. *Power* is the morality of men who stand out from the rest, and it is also mine.' "

After he became deaf, he became defiant:

" 'I will take Fate by the throat,' he said. He was, as it were, *defending* his creative power. But by the end of this summer he found that his genius, that he had felt called on to cherish and protect, was really a mighty force using him as a channel or servant. . . . But only when the consciously defiant Beethoven had succumbed, only when his pride and strength had been so reduced that he was willing, even eager, to die and abandon the struggle, did he find that his creative power was indeed indestructible and that it was its deathless energy that made it impossible for him to die. . . . Never again was his attitude towards life one of defiance, . . . for he no longer had any fear. He had become aware within himself of an indomitable creative energy that nothing could destroy. . . . His realization of the deep-rooted character of his own creative power . . . changed the character of the problem of his attitude towards life. A rigid, strained defiance was no longer necessary. What he came to see as his most urgent task, for his future spiritual development, was *submission*. He had to learn to accept suffering as in some mysterious way necessary."

This conviction is evidenced by an entry in his journal:

" 'Submission, absolute submission, to your fate, only this can give you the sacrifice. . . . Thou mayest no longer be a man, not for thyself, only for others, for thee there is no longer happiness except in . . . thy art . . . O God, give me strength to conquer myself, nothing must chain me to life.'

"Beethoven's profoundest attitude towards life, as expressed in his music, owes nothing to the mediation of his intelligence. The synthesis of his experience that is achieved by a great artist proceeds according to laws of which we know almost nothing, but purely intellectual formulation plays a very small part in it. If Beethoven reached the state, as we believe he did, where he achieved the 'submission' he felt to be so necessary, it was not through any process of reasoning."[4]

In the climb towards alignment, it is as if we are met along the road:

". . . the instant one sets out in quest of Jesus, one has found Him, since He is the Condition which makes such a search possible. He is Spirit and the moment we become spectators and critics of ourselves, we take our stand in the realm of Spirit. The first step in our ascent is thereby accomplished."[5]

Alignment will not lessen your problems, spare you agony, free you from encounters with catastrophe or crisis. On the contrary, it will intensify your own suffering and broaden the area of your sensitivity to the sufferings of others. Alignment is no formula for exempting. But unless you ignore history you will discover that people who know where they are going, unlike the purposeless and directionless millions and all who have lost their way, these are the happy people. Even in ordeal they are happy people, no longer demanding to bargain with fate or to be released from ordeal as a condition of living splendidly—and splendour can be a quality of living.

You will discover, too, that *your* way, at last known beyond all guessing, is revealed stage by stage, *as you need it to be*. Controlled as by the pole star, certainty of direction becomes clear. Faltering, stumbling, battered, scarred, always you will find your way back, not because you know more, but because knowing has become receiving, your own will being now of no account. It isn't that this is a better way. It has become your only way. No essential need for allegiance to creed or dogma—you will use them if they support you and reject them if they are chains—allegiance is to that highest self, the element of the divine in every one of us, which is the ego's enemy. The conflict of loyalties solved, you are equipped to come through loneliness, pain and terror.

This way is not labelled "happiness." Planning for happiness is planning for a mirage. Happiness remains a by-product, some-times fleeting as a moment, yet it can become a lasting benison.

They attain to it who plan for something worth while, not consciously related to their own happiness. This is the responding to something which impels man to aim higher than his best, that intertwining of the human with the divine which is so baffling to the logical mind.

# XIV

## AFTERWARDS

I believe that another world than this exists, and that the door which shuts upon this life opens upon a wider one. So I think it is necessary not to cling too much to old memories, which generally become worn and out of date. They are only signposts.—For there seems no reason to suppose that there is no continuity, no progress, when once one has stepped outside Time. Our lives are the threads in a vast pattern, and Time the shuttle which links us all together in eternity. It is only we, within our finite minds, who feel that nothing is possible outside the world we know. Only by stretching our minds in silence towards God can we hope to reach Him, and through Him, the ones we love. But that is a silent and a private journey.

"Marraine"
(a pen-portrait of Yvonne Arnaud)
by her god-daughter Oriel Malet

HAMMER AND ANVIL, potter and clay, sculptor and stone—out of the hammering and the fire, the moulding and the hard chiselling, something takes shape. But in the shaping of humanity and the conditioning of the person for specific purposes, more than this is required, something more, even, than destiny; it is co-operation. As St. Augustine put it, "Without God, we cannot; without us, He will not."

The ordeal confirmed my belief in that.

Out of the crucible emerges something different from what went in. Ordeal by fire changes us. The crucible's scorch disposes of much clutter; much that you thought important is proved to be almost irrelevant and you are ready to discard it. Ordeal clears your vision, changes your valuations; you come to distinguish with fair accuracy between time frittered away and time used wisely. "An educated man," wrote Dr. Albert Mansbridge, founder of the Workers' Educational Association, "is one who uses time aright,"[1] "Aright" includes doing nothing, and may include much of it—indeed this can be vital in "becoming" rather than "achieving" but it is the opposite of the wasting of time and the impatiently filled gaps, and the excess time consumed by trivialities and by the mechanics of living. So cleansing is ordeal that once you have seen the light, you always know when you are slithering, and there is no escape, you are no longer unsure.

As if to complement this, you become more sure about compassion, its being perhaps the most urgent, the deepest, the most widespread human need at a stage of history when man has lost his way; an age of loneliness. Due to ordeal, your sympathy acquires the compelling reality of compassion, a crying urge bequeathed out of your experience, and in particular, a yearning to share with the bereaved for whom, for whatever reasons, tranquillity has not emerged, those whose memories are an emotional wear and tear, often seeming to be essential evidence of loyalty, often deferring hard-won peace. In its humility, your never-questioning compassion goes out to all who would transmute emotional turmoil into harmony. How difficult it is, to treat the past wisely, to realize that life is today, *today only*, irradiated by all the yesterdays from which we have shed the morbid and the haunting.

Ordeal can bring serenity which you long to share; with infinite tenderness you would help resenting sufferers to escape from their imprisoning bitterness, emancipated, their restless minds at last stilled, to discover that stillness can become an adventuring into creative acceptance. Whatever is creative can bring zest. "Creative" implies the objective view, a focus on something other than one's self, a renunciation. Instead of brooding, beckoning; tomorrow no longer feared; tomorrow to be the maturing of the yesterdays into deeper tranquillity. Instead of tortured longings for the irretrievable past, dragging and futile, the vitality of new dawns bracing one for welcomed horizons. The road to these horizons is a road leading out of loneliness.

This needs time, long or short, varying from those whose way is arduous to those privileged to visualize near horizons clear of fog, unclouded by emotional turmoil. It needs discipline, too. Fidelity to the pole star; no flinching, no swerving—impossible save for the patterning made for you, which you dare not forget. The discipline may become dedication, even if it is never complete; for you will falter and stumble, but always the discipline of shedding, then pushing ahead; exhausted and sometimes felled to the ground, then somehow scrambling forward, wasting never a moment on the contemplation of failure, which is only part of the road, encouraging you, if you interpret it wisely, to tread more firmly, eyes and mind on the climb, never on the stumbling.

My personal position seemed highly privileged. At first, no sign came, that the harmony would continue. How dare one guess that harmony wrung from distress, suffering and sacrifice would not be broken? I had no plans. Two years of "one day at a time" had convinced me that whilst no plans could have meaning, the wise future would gradually unfold. This kind of faith can be born out of endurance and out of thick fog which envelops even the near stretch of the road, the discipline of the days equipping one to stop battering at tomorrow's door.

The onset of the disease had come at a time when vaguely, we were becoming aware of the possibility of retirement, that heavenly anticipatory phase in which you begin to realize that business can become a treadmill; involuntarily, you find yourself scanning advertisements of country cottages, and wondering. London, when you have come to love its infinity of moods and the diversity of its offerings, could one—dare one, leave it, coming back only rarely? For the countryside of yesterday is today's suburbia; how far must one go to avoid possible daily invasion by a sky-full of helicopter-commuters?

As it turned out, the end of Dorfs' ordeal was for me the heralding of a new quest; the completeness of her alignment had changed my world. The house acquired bequeathed serenity; moving to a country cottage, or moving anywhere, would have seemed, and still would seem, to be banishment. This was indeed continuity; in the years since Dorfs died there has been no moment when continuity has been broken. "Death is too slight a thing," wrote a friend, "to separate those who really love each other." This is so true that it can free us from bondage: "Death is *too slight a thing* to separate those who really love each other."

Two problems confront the honest searcher. First, the physical. Nothing can bring back the *physical* person we knew. All our longing for irretrievable yesterdays, so understandable, our yearnings, deep and so sincere, how shall we escape from them —ever? *And wouldn't it be disloyal,* if we could? And the answer is that thousands of the bereaved are living proof that it is not only possible and wise—it is the one way to fulfil responsibilities which make our personal yearnings seem almost self-indulgent. This is stern. Psychiatrists and psychologists, priests and physicians all know of the healing way into which stern discipline can lead. They know, too, the wisest of them, how important it is to focus on something positive instead of brooding on something negative:

> ". . . Invalids
> using a language full of woefulness
> to tell us where it hurts, instead of sternly
> transforming into words those selves of theirs,
> as imperturbable cathedral carvers
> transported themselves into the constant stone."[2]

At this point, we have to avoid intruding on those who completely rule out the possibility of anything following this present life. If you are utterly, finally convinced that death is the end of everything, the most that this chapter has any right to do is to record the convictions of the multitude who do not believe that. They include, in addition to those who believe in re-incarnation, those who claim to have been in contact with departed loved ones, and those by whom "messages" are said to have been received, a vast mass of people who believe that to imagine death as finality doesn't make sense. They include those of us who are content with belief in a mystery beyond the capacity of our minds to penetrate, a mystery revealed to love with clarity and certainty, no longer demanding definition by the brain, which has here no authority, no way of helping; important to avoid confusing its realm with the realm of the spirit. This is holy ground.

If then, we are willing to believe that in some way beyond our understanding, death is not the end of everything, it is not unreasonable to think of the physical body as clothing and equipment needed for the chapter which is this life, a chapter and not the whole story. Discarding the clothing and equipment at the end of the chapter can be seen as a necessary, obvious process, evidence that whatever the nature and conditions of the next chapter, this clothing, this equipment is not required. If that is so, it becomes easier to contemplate a loved one *going on to something*, instead of being deprived of something.

Here we link up with the second problem confronting the honest searcher—time. If life here is a chapter instead of a completed book, something must follow. Recognition that death is not the end of everything implies some kind of continuity, either a further stretch of time, comprehensible to the mind, or eternity, the very nature of which is beyond human guessing. Believing that one chapter must lead to whatever is the next chapter, do the terms matter very much, save to theologians and scientists? And since we have little beyond conjecture to guide us, isn't it enough to be content with the belief in something continuing instead of something ending; to be aware of the need for mystery? Wise men know that there are many things which can never be explained, nor does the welcomed acceleration of scientific achievement affect the mysteries relating to the human spirit, a field in which it is almost powerless to operate. And since man's spirit is committed to an ultimate search for peace, mystery, which is one of its approaches, is a surer way than the fruitless arguments, puzzling those who would like to penetrate the impenetrable, bewildering to each succeeding generation.

How privileged I was, I could realize only gradually. There was never the "vacant chair." Light,—pervading, effulgent light, was everywhere. Peace was tranquillity, as it had been for so long. In this place I could do happily whatever I might be required to do in the partnership. The home would continue to radiate the light which Dorfs had received, radiated, given to it. In stepping into my new life there had been no moment of misgiving. All had continued positive and sure. Nor had anything disturbed my assurance that as each new day came, the plan for the day would unfold. My freedom to reject any plan continued to spur me, not into the confidence of the conqueror, but into the urge of the pilgrim, aware of the painful slowness of such progress as can be shown when the slippings and the failures and all the indulgence are deducted from the reckoning. Never had I lost direction. Lost myself, yes, often, submerged in one or other of the manifestations of self-indulgence. But at no time had direction been lost—or the deep, overwhelming desire to maintain it. Beyond the daily plan there would somehow, some day, emerge a pattern. I knew that. Too often, striving too hard, I wanted to examine the detail of the pattern. Then I was forced into recognition of the futility of the striving. The "lilies of the field" had to be remembered, not once, but on many a day when I so impetuously wanted to get ahead, to press on in top gear.

Gradually, the inevitability of time became so accepted that I lost my impatience; I was ready to go much more slowly than I had felt I ought to be going. My experience seemed to be fundamentally different from the Damascus Road experience of St. Paul, struck down, blinded, a changed man. Nothing remotely corresponding to that had happened to me. The analogy was in the aftermath. St. Paul, also impetuous, wanted to get ahead at once in the new pattern of his living, but for a long time, a very long time, he had to be quietly schooled. So had I. Around the phrase "work out your own salvation" the pattern began to take definite shape; all over again, and with new certainty, I realized that if we are determined to follow whatever patterning we honestly believe to be inevitable for us, then we can order our living in ways which will prevent anything on earth from hindering us.

Once you are sure, your pattern will bring joy and laughter as well as nearly every form of discouragement and near-failure; much that seemed worth while will be jettisoned as tawdry or shoddy or stupid; so many things will acquire new meaning, and if you are fortunate, some of them will be simple, unsophisticated things, as simple as those recorded in this immortal passage:

"You never enjoy the world aright, till the sea itself floweth in your veins, till you are clothed with the heavens, and crowned with the stars: and perceive yourself to be the sole heir of the whole world, and more so, because men are in it who are every one sole heirs with you. Till you can sing and rejoice and delight in God, as misers do in gold, and Kings in sceptres, you never enjoy the world."[3]

This is the rhythm of freedom; freedom gained through simplifying. A dozen years before she died, Dorfs wrote to a friend who needed guidance: "Live simply, think simply, breathe deeply, and lift up your heart." In this uncomplicated creed, she had always believed; evidence of the infectious gaiety of her philosophy which was becoming for me a dominant influence as well as an inspiration. Inactivity was no longer a gap; it was quiet, and sometimes it was stillness. Shedding more and more, like shedding dead leaves, I was—as later I realized—surrendering as she had surrendered into whatever might become the future.

Some who are bereaved may have to learn new ways of dealing with loneliness. Loneliness there may never be, if by the combination of grace and self-discipline we are brought into the new chapter sufficiently free from emotional ravages to see the new horizons, which cannot be the same as the old horizons. The old horizons can hold us, and hold us back. New horizons beckon us. Life means going forward. When the forward impulse in us begins to weaken, vitality weakens, the vitality that is life itself. Unless we come to a new interpretation of the old relationship, making it a vibrant sharing of a continuing partnership, we risk the fading of the vision. Living in the past may be consoling; it cannot be energizing. Instead of the treasured physical image only, the new interpretation can comprise all that the personality embodied in courage, calmness, gaiety of spirit, all becoming as vital as personality can be, the remembered physical image no longer seeming to draw us back but to propel us into our new world with the courage of two instead of the courage of one.

This is partnership indeed. It is the disciplined resolve to build a new life on the foundations of the old one. Instead of "I have to go on living," new, shared living can be an exciting, daily recurring opportunity, for building is an exciting occupation. Especially if you focus on something more than building for yourself. You may lose yourself, the simplest, surest way of finding yourself. The emotional chains can then fall off. In new-found activities, hobbies and many new interests, some of them creative, you are emancipated from the emotional drenchings in which you could so easily founder, longing not to be rescued, but to be submerged. Disillusionment and mistakes and failures continue as long as life, but your new-found equipment to resist, to overcome and stride forward, means that you will be battle-scarred but never completely overwhelmed. You are remembering that there can be wise forgetting, and this helps to put remorse in its right place; for remorse may have a place. Facing the recollection that there are so many things you might have done better, so many hurtful things you should not have done, you have to use your new equipment to avoid wallowing in remorse, pure self-indulgence. Remorse has to be creative. It can heal, when the focus is away from the self. "Remorse," wrote Dorfs, many years before her last illness, "is salvation, provided it is later translated into an experience from which we equip ourselves for right living." Focus not on guilt, but on opportunity; creating this kind of opportunity and using it fully solves one of the psychiatrist's sinister problems—the problem of self-forgiveness, which can block the way ahead. We have to be generous with ourselves. Gentleness with ourselves need not be self-indulgence.

In our wise forgetting we come to forget the suffering, the frustrations, the pain and distress—they can no longer invade and destroy the tranquillity which we need as we strive to build a new life. "She is only through the door, in the next room," a friend remarked, on hearing that Dorfs had died; how tragic, had I pictured her continuing to suffer.

". . . human hearts disdain to quit their woe,
Hug fast their tempests, love their knife-edge winds."[4]

What has been achieved by handicapped people, by all who have suffered and endured, by all the wounded spirits, this constitutes a responsibility for us as we become torch-bearers. For a while, we are on the stage, compelled to play a part. Our stewardship responsibility is unavoidable.

There may be something in the idea that the universe began to take shape as a thought in the mind of God. Life is renewal and creation, the creation of the universe, more and more generally regarded as a continuing process.

Our influence may be more potent than we have imagined; choosing its nature, its character, is part of the inescapable burden of our free-will. Rebellion against the best in us is the road to loneliness, anxiety and despair. Co-operation is the road to hope, and hope is a dawn.

# NOTES

## CHAPTER I

1. *The Donnellan Lectures*, p. 65, Lord Dunsany.

## CHAPTER III

1. *Divine Healing and Co-operation between Doctors and Clergy* (British Medical Association).
2. From a letter dated 1948, referred to in *God and the Unconscious*, by Victor White, O.P. (Collins).
3. From *A Theory of Disease*, by Dr. Arthur Guirdham (George Allen & Unwin).
4. *Nursing Times* pamphlet—reprint of articles.
5. *Some Thoughts on Faith Healing* (Tyndale Press).
6. *Eminent Victorians*, by Lytton Strachey (Chatto & Windus).

## CHAPTER IV

1. *Frontier*, Spring 1963. R. A. Lambourne, M.B., Ch.B. (Christian Frontier Council).
2. *Freedom and the Spirit*, p. 46, Berdyaev (Geoffrey Bles).
3. *Recovery of Faith*, p. 188, Radhakrishnan (George Allen & Unwin).
4. *The Cloud of Unknowing*, Penguin edition, p. 55.
5. *The Son's Course*, Intro., p. 9, Gerald Vann (Collins).
6. *Memories, Dreams, Reflections*, p. 328, Carl Jung (Collins).
7. Titus, chap. 3, v. 10 (J. B. Phillips translation) (Geoffrey Bles).

## CHAPTER V

1. *De Profundis*, p. 82, p. 78, p. 114, p. 68 (Methuen).
2. *I Leap Over the Wall*, p. 252, Monica Baldwin (Hamish Hamilton).
3. Ann Armstrong to the author, December 18th, 1962.

### CHAPTER VI

1. *Determined to Live*, p. 160, Rev. Brian Hession (Peter Davies).
2. *London Calling*, July 4th, 1946. (B.B.C. Publications).
3. *Imitation of Christ* (Penguin edition), pp. 80 and 101, Thomas à Kempis.

### CHAPTER VII

1. "The Eve of St. Agnes", John Keats.
2. *The Times*, January 25th, 1962.
3. Luke, chap. 10, v. 27.
4. *Man: The Forgotten*, p. 37 (Sheed & Ward).
5. *The Faith and Practice of the Quakers*, pp. 3-6, Rufus M. Jones (Methuen).
6. Comment printed on the fly-leaf of Rufus Jones' book, *The Faith and Practice of the Quakers* (Methuen).
7. *President Masaryk tells his Story*, p. 215, President Masaryk (George Allen & Unwin).
8. *Image Old and New*, p. 14 (S.P.C.K.).
9. *Christian Apologetics*, p. 243 (S.C.M. Press).
10. *A Time to Keep Silence*, p. 39 (John Murray).

### CHAPTER VIII

1. *George Macdonald, An Anthology*, C. S. Lewis (Geoffrey Bles).
2. *This I Believe*, p. 140 (Hamish Hamilton).
3. *My Apprenticeship*, Penguin edition, Vol. I, p. 126, Beatrice Webb.
4. *Retreats Today*. Published by the Association for Promoting Retreats.
5. *Spiritual Letters* (Sheed & Ward).
6. *Life of St. Teresa*, Penguin edition, p. 158.
7. *The Teachings of the Mystics*, pp. 151 and 153 (Harper & Row).

### CHAPTER IX

1. Quoted in *World Faiths*, September, 1961 (World Congress of Faiths).

2. Introduction to *The Song of God*—a new translation (Chatto & Windus).
3. *Readings in St. John's Gospel*, Intro., p. xxx (Macmillan).
4. Article in the *Observer*, January 1st, 1963.
5. Introduction to *The Phenomenon of Man* (Collins).

### CHAPTER X

1. *Spiritual Letters*, p. 313, Dom John Chapman (Sheed & Ward).
2. *The Age of Chivalry*, p. 465, Sir Arthur Bryant (Collins).
3. *Le Milieu Divin*, p. 39, Pierre Teilhard de Chardin (Collins).
4. *Science of Thought Review*, December, 1958, Clare Cameron.
5. *My Search for Truth*, Chapter 13 (Science of Thought Press).
6. *My Search for Truth*, Chapter 17 (Science of Thought Press).

### CHAPTER XII

1. *The Wandering Scholars*, p. 11 (Constable).
2. *Freedom of the Spirit*, p. 150, Berdyaev (Geoffrey Bles).
3. "Bishop Blougram's Apology", Robert Browning.
4. *Self-Abandonment to Divine Providence*, p. 23, P. de Caussade (Burns & Oates).

### CHAPTER XIII

1. Quoted from *Frontier*, Spring 1962 (Christian Frontier Council).
2. *William Temple*, p. 503, F. A. Iremonger (Oxford University Press).
3. Penguin edition.
4. Penguin edition.
5. *Pascal and the Mystical Tradition*, p. 102, F. T. H. Fletcher (Basil Blackwell & Mott).

### CHAPTER XIV

1. Address at Pittsburgh University, June 1927.
2. *Requiem*, Intro., p. 46, Rainer Maria Rilke (Hogarth Press).
3. *Centuries of Meditations*, p. 19, Thomas Traherne (Dobell).
4. Pearl Adam in a book of poems printed for private circulation.